The First Congregational Church of Woodbury, Connecticut:
350 Years of Faith, Fellowship, and Service

Sarah K. Griswold,
Stephen P. McGrath

authorHOUSE®

First Congregational Church and Ecclesiastical Society of Woodbury, Connecticut

AuthorHouse™
1663 Liberty Drive
Bloomington, IN 47403
www.authorhouse.com
Phone: 1 (800) 839-8640

Published by AuthorHouse 07/02/2020

ISBN: 978-1-7283-5999-1 (sc)
ISBN: 978-1-7283-5998-4 (e)

Library of Congress Control Number: 2020907384

Print information available on the last page.

DEDICATION

This book is dedicated to all the faithful members of the First Congregational Church and Ecclesiastical Society, living and departed, who have served, supported, and loved her for 350 years.

PREFACE

At the writing of this history, the future of the First Congregational Church is uncertain. Faced with changing local demographics and dwindling membership, exacerbated by national trends, the church voted in the fall of 2019 to suspend worship services at the end of May, 2020. coincident with the 350th anniversary of its founding.

As tragic as this is, and as contingent as the future may be, something had to be done to recognize the long and noble history of First Church and the role it has played in founding and shaping the community that is Woodbury. To this end, member for 45 years, Linda Osterman Hamid conceived the idea of this book, and her beloved friend David Sonnemann, a member of North Congregational Church, stepped forward and offered to support such an effort financially. It is due to their inspiration, devotion and generosity that this book is made possible.

Creating this book meant starting, literally, from scratch. The previous volume, which had been authored by Marion Mabey in 1994, covered the church from its founding in Stratford as the Second Congregational Society to the end of the 18th Century. Its focus was primarily on the theological controversies that shaped the early church. Since Mrs. Mabey's book, however, nothing had been done to present the church's history in the 19th and 20th Centuries.

All the material lay in the archives of the church, basically in four large file drawers containing hundreds of documents and fragments of information. We have had to peruse all these bits and pieces, make judgments about what was most important to include and what wasn't, and organize a history that would tell an interesting story while remaining faithful to the evidence. To all this written documentation, we added interviews with several parishioners and clergy, past and present, to shed light on the church in more recent times. Understanding that each comes with a unique perspective, we have tried to balance and weigh these in shaping our narrative.

We had been given less than a year to research and write this book, which is a short time for an undertaking of this magnitude, so the reader will not be surprised to find that we have left things out that might have been included, but which would have made meeting our deadline impossible. Many of the topics presented here could be separate articles or books in themselves. For example, much more could be done with the efforts of the brave young missionary women that this church raised up and sent out to distant corners of the globe and to the United States itself. Armed only with their undaunted courage and Christian faith, these women carried what they had learned at First Church to others who had not been so fortunate. And some gave their lives in those efforts. The parish records have a treasure-trove of information on this topic and many others that future historians may explore in greater depth. Moreover, special recognition goes to Maria Platt, Church Administrator, and Linda Osterman Hamid, for their invaluable work on the photographs.

It is our hope that, whether tomorrow or one hundred years from now, the reader will begin to understand something of the long and storied history of First Church and that the legacy of First Church transcends the passing of the ages.

Sarah K. Griswold   Stephen P. McGrath

INTRODUCTION

"Liberty to Erect a Plantation at Pomperaug"

The history of First Church is a story that rests on its own, but we must remember that it also reflects the larger stories of our town, state, region, nation, and world. At no time have the parishioners of the church existed outside the larger framework of history and society. The church has evolved over its 350 years, reflecting the changing society around it, and in no small part, contributing to those changes, if only as a part of the larger story.

Woodbury's history stretches back at least 10,000 years. With the recent discovery of 13,500 year old remains in Avon, it seems certain that indigenous people were in our area then as well. Although dismissed as "savages" by the European settlers who displaced them, current research and the testimony of indigenous peoples who remain teach us that theirs was a sophisticated and sustainable way of life, well worthy of the respect that it is belatedly getting.

Our story, however, starts with the settlement of these native lands by the English settlers from Stratford, Connecticut, who, driven both by doctrine and practical needs, made their way up the Housatonic River to the Pomperaug River (by way of the larger Shepaug River), and settled in a fertile valley that had already been cleared and farmed by the native Pootatucks.

Although the settlers purchased their land, it should be noted that the concept of property ownership was radically different for Native and English peoples, and reflected an almost insurmountable misunderstanding that resulted in the disenfranchisement and loss of cultural identity for the Native people. However, it should also be noted that it did not mean that these people simply disappeared. Even in the church records Native people are recognized, if only fleetingly.

Connecticut's settlement by Europeans began, briefly, in settlements by the Dutch, although the major permanent European settlements began in the 1630s, with the arrival of the English. Settlers went to Windsor and Wethersfield in 1633 and 1634; Thomas Hooker came to Hartford in 1636. Other settlers went to Old Saybrook in 1635 and New Haven in 1638. These three territories were initially separate colonies that were joined together as a colony of the English Crown in 1662.

Stratford had been founded in 1639. It was in May, 1670, that a committee composed of Mr. Sherman, Mr. Fayrechild, Lieutenant Curtiss, Ensign Judson, Mr. Hawley, and John Minor who had proposed to buy land in 1667, was granted permission to do so. This parcel was known as Pomperaug, named after a sachem of the Potatucks. On May 9, 1672, the court granted Samuel Sherman, William Curtiss, Joseph Judson, and John Minor permission to "erect a plantation at Pomperaug, with the direction that they settle there within three years. Fifteen men of Mr. Walker's congregation arrived with their families in the early spring of 1673. "[1] This was the first settlement of Europeans in this part of the state, and was a mere four decades after the first incursions by them.

---

[1] William Cothren, <u>History of Ancient Woodbury, Vol.</u> I, (Waterbury Conn.: J. Seeley and Sons, 1871) 33-34

As Marion Mabey narrates in her 1994 work on the history of the church, the origins of the First Congregational Church of Woodbury lay in the theological disputes of mid-17th Century Puritan New England. Before 1662, membership in a Puritan church was determined by vote of the congregation, based upon applicants for membership testifying publicly that they had a 'conversion' experience. This involved a period of prayer and inner reflection, a sense of one's own depravity and total reliance on God's grace for salvation, and a willingness to amend their lives and live according to the discipline of the church. If the congregation judged a conversion to be authentic, the applicant was voted in; if not, the applicant was excluded until a more authentic conversion could be recounted.

As the second generation of Puritans grew to maturity, fewer and fewer could testify to a conversion experience, and by 1660 nearly half of those who had been baptized as infants and attended church every Sunday were not admitted to Communion because they lacked the requisite conversion. They were, in effect, half way or non-communicating, church attendees. The most knotty question emerged when these families brought their children for Baptism, and the issue of whether children of non-church members could be baptized rocked both Connecticut and Massachusetts.

In a meeting at Cambridge, the Massachusetts clergy worked out a compromise, often termed the "Half Way Covenant" and formulated it into a policy statement known as the Cambridge Platform. This allowed the children of those who had been baptized but never admitted to full communion to have their own children baptized.

Individual churches were given the freedom to adopt the Half-Way Covenant or not. Many Connecticut churches adopted it, but the stern, Calvinist minister at the First Church of Stratford, Israel Chauncey, refused to allow it. Dissidents formed their own congregation, endorsed the Half-Way Covenant, chose their own pastor, Zechariah Walker, and appealed to the legislature for redress. A time-sharing agreement between the church and the dissident congregation was brokered, which ultimately proved unsatisfactory. After an appeal to the General Court (colony legislature), the dissident congregation was granted permission to form the Second Society of Stratford in 1670 and granted permission in 1674 to move the congregation in its entirety to create a settlement along the Pomperaug River in what is today Woodbury.

The fledgling settlement held services at Bethel Rock in good weather, and in private homes (such as they were) in winter. By 1681, the church was ready to erect its new meeting house in what is now the south end of town, across from Drum Rock, where a drummer would call the congregants to Sunday meeting.

For much of the 18th Century, the church was led by Anthony Stoddard, son of the great New England theologian Solomon Stoddard of Northampton, Massachusetts[2], who developed the liberal practice of extending Communion to half-way members, hoping to lead them to full membership. Anthony Stoddard implemented this practice in Woodbury, which in practice broke down the spiritual distinction between full and half-way members. The distinction then became one of politics: only full members could serve as deacons or on the board of the Ecclesiastical Society. First Church, then, would have been considered a "liberal" church in those days.

As the western sector of Connecticut grew in population after 1700, First Church of Woodbury founded several daughter churches in the newly-formed surrounding towns: Southbury (1730); Bethlehem (1739); Judea (later Washington) (1741); Roxbury (1743) and South Britain (1766).

By mid-century, however, the religious unity of Woodbury itself was disrupted by the growing influence of the Anglican Church in Connecticut. A small group of First Church members formed an Anglican Church, later

---

[2] Solomon Stoddard was the grandfather of Jonathan Edwards, the great theologian of the the 18th century and generally considered to be America's first philosopher. Edwards was also the grandfather of Aaron Burr, Jr., Vice President of the US under Jefferson, and the man who shot Alexander Hamilton in a duel.

named St. Paul's, stepping outside the town's historic religious consensus. Despite their positions on opposite sides during the American Revolution, the two churches quickly developed amicable relations after the War, and First Church gave a parcel of its cemetery land to the Anglicans for their church building. It was, incidentally, at a meeting in the Glebe House (the Anglican minister's house) that the Connecticut Anglican clergy chose Reverend Mr. Samuel Seabury to be the first bishop of the Protestant Episcopal Church in Connecticut.[3]

---

[3] The information for this Introduction has been liberally taken from Marion Mabey, A History of the First Congregational Church of Woodbury, Connecticut (1994) This was privately published. John G. Fleming and Judith M. Plummer published the manuscript as far as Dr. Mabey was able to go before her death. Mabey's work is quite good, especially on the theological controversies of the day.

TRANSCENDENTLY BEAUTIFUL: THE THREE BUILDINGS OF FIRST CHURCH

A common thought currently in vogue is that the practice of Christianity does not depend on buildings but on actions. The maintenance of a large, wooden building certainly requires constant attention and expense that can seem to divert attention away from the spiritual in favor of roofing, drains, and paint. Religious history is full of instances where the form has overtaken the practice and the 'vanities of this world' have come to replace the awareness of the Divine. In fact the rise of Puritanism was partly in response to the material excesses of the Roman Catholic Church.

However, humans have always gravitated to finding or making places where the Sacred can be approached, honored, appealed to, and learned from. The acknowledgment of a sacred space can be a pile of stones or a cave or a temple; it can be in the center of a settlement or in an inaccessible corner depending on the belief system of the culture, but it is always somewhere, and that somewhere is important. This is as true in Woodbury as anywhere.

In our Congregational tradition, especially in the early, Puritan days, the church building not only served as a place where people could meet together for both secular and sacred purposes, it also reflected theological and social ideas that underpinned their social interactions, their family relations, their moral engagement, and their fundamental understanding of the best way to be in this world. The structure and the placement of the place of worship were very important.

Today we think the meaning of a building is found less in its structure, design, and siting and more in the activities that take place within it. This is a recent development, born of changes in theology, the way a particular religious practice exists in ever-more diverse communities, and the ease with which buildings can now be erected. Modern church building sometimes references traditional elements such as a church spire, but rarely uses those elements to underline theology or practice. But for the Puritans and their descendants in the 17th, 18th, and into the 19th centuries, the form and location of the building spoke volumes to its people and the community at large. Thus, tracing the development of the buildings of First Church is an important subject of study in its own right, and mirrors the changes in the denomination and in society at large.

The current church building is the third of the Society; the first two are now lost, except, possibly, recycled as timbers in other buildings. Detailed descriptions or representations of these buildings don't exist, but some information has been passed along that allows us to know something about them. And the forms of the buildings in Woodbury follow the forms that were contemporary at the time of their erection.

Almost ten years after settlement, in 1681, the first meeting house was built near the intersection of Hollow Road and Main Street, near the cliffs of the current Masonic Temple. As mentioned earlier, until then members had met in each other's houses or at Bethel Rock, a cliff formation that is part of the Orenaug rocks (and near the Masonic Temple cliffs) and an outstanding physical feature of the town. Tradition maintains that in the early days a drummer would stand on these cliffs to call worshipers to meetings. This was a fairly standard practice in Puritan villages.

The building was said to be square and large[4], which would be in keeping with standard practice of the time. The overall aesthetics of these early churches reflected the theology of the worshippers. For these Protestants, hearing the Word was central to worship. Unlike the interiors of the Anglican and Catholic churches of Britain and Europe, with their vaulted ceilings and windows that lead the eye upward, open naves allowing for movement, and a liturgical focus to worship, the Protestant church interior focused on the pulpit, where minister and deacons read scripture, prayed, and preached. Box pews were closely built around and focused on the pulpit and seats in them were assigned according to rank. The space was closely defined, linear, and well lighted, the communion table movable rather than being a fixed altar, the ceiling low and the pulpit elaborate.[5] There may have been galleries or seats along the walls for children, servants, and people of color to sit on.

In his book Architecture and Town Planning in Connecticut," Anthony Garvan points out what he calls "the poverty of [Connecticut's] public architecture." Between the work needed to establish communities and the status of the land as a colony with the locus of government in England, "the Crown felt no obligation to initiate large scale building…the seventeenth century in Connecticut was an age of modest meetinghouses and comfortable homes."[6]

> Perhaps this very absence of monumental architecture contrived to focus the town's attention on its first meetinghouse to a degree that few of its larger and more handsome successors enjoyed. In most towns it occupied the central site, and its early erection was a matter of pride. Within its walls not only Sunday worship but also much

[4] J. Frederick Kelly, Early Connecticut Meeting Houses (New York: Columbia University Press, 1948), 19

[5] Garvan, 130.

[6] *Ibid.*

town business was conducted… Religious architecture in New England can best be understood as an offshoot of the European Plain Style which in England, Holland, Germany, and Huguenot France answered the militant challenge of Catholic architecture… Without liturgy, ornament, or monumental scale, in the simplest of interiors they managed to present a clear reasoned solution for their house of prayer.[7]

The Meeting House was used not only for church services, but as a meeting house for town affairs. As Edward F. Rines puts it "The meeting house in early Puritan settlements, while primarily utilized as a place of worship, was generally employed also to serve the educational and political needs of the community.…These meetings were always opened by prayer and not infrequently a sermon was included for good measure. The men attending these meetings did not remove their hats or make any effort to modulate their voices or modify their demeanor for the "Puritan did not reverence the meeting house as a structure, though he was punctilious in honoring it when it was used for the worship of God.""[8]

Woodbury's humble but proud building saw the end of Reverend Walker's tenure and the beginning of Anthony Stoddard's. It was used for sixty-six years, until the second meeting house, started in 1744, was completed in 1747.

Peter T. Mallary writes "The end of the seventeenth century saw the New England Way, if not in disarray, at least somewhat disheveled. The heart of seventeenth-century life had been the Word. The eighteenth saw earthly pursuits demand equal status with spiritual clarity."[9] Mallary points out that people started to outgrow towns and the diversifying of

[7] *Ibid.*

[8] Old Historic Churches of America, Their Romantic History and Traditions, (New York:The Macmillan Company, 1936)

[9] Peter T. Mallary, New England Churches and Meeting Houses,(Boston: Chartwell Books, 1985) *passim.*

economic pursuits and settlers meant that it was no longer quite possible to control people as it had been when the culture was more localized and homogenous. In addition, the pastors were beginning to lose their unquestioned civic as well as moral power.[10]

In Woodbury, the pressures of earthly pursuits were certainly being felt. As the earliest town in this part of Connecticut, Woodbury was well established and thriving. It was the seat of the probate court and a center of transportation networks. These factors, with the addition of the parishes being settled all around it and bringing surplus goods to town, led to Woodbury becoming a significant market town. A class of men developed who assumed control of the trade. They were not all church members; the best known, perhaps, was Jabez Bacon, who never had a clear ecclesiastical affiliation. The town had grown dramatically after 1730. In 1748 the town petitioned the General Assembly to form a separate county for southern Litchfield County, with Woodbury as its seat. By 1774, Woodbury's tax index was by far the highest in Litchfield County, far outstripping Litchfield.[11]

With the growth of the town and increased prosperity came two pressures. One was to build a meeting house more worthy of the new status of the town as a force to be reckoned with in the Colony, and the population growth that followed it. The other, related pressure, was to start to relax the doctrinal code by which the church organized itself, to begin to evolve in favor of the growing heterogeneity of the burgeoning colony. This second pressure was not a development that was limited to Woodbury, by any means, and throughout New England the 'meeting house plan' was giving way to the 'church plan.' Whereas the meeting house plan had the entry on the short axis of the building and the pulpit, facing the entrance,

---

[10] See Ann Douglas The Feminization of American Culture (New York: Farrar, Straus and Giroux,) for an excellent review of the dynamics of this power shift
[11] Edward S. Cooke, Jr. Fiddlebacks and Crooked-backs, (Waterbury, Conn:Mattatuck Historical Society, 1982)

the central focus of attention around which the box pews were organized, the church plan placed the entrance doors on the gable end of the building with the pulpit at the far end of the auditorium, still facing the doors, but in a design that moves the eye forward and up. The bell towers were becoming steeples. At least according to the illustration provided in William Cothren's *History of Ancient Woodbury,* the second meeting house seems to have been a transitional form, with the bell tower and steeple on the gable, or short end, of the church and a single door in the center of the tower, and the main door on the long side of the building. Although the church records before 1770 have long been lost, a vote to shut the steeple door as soon as worship begins seems to bear this out. Other references suggest that there was a central alley, with additional aisles on the west and east sides.

[Second Meeting-House.]

Second Building Built 1747

6

Joseph Minor, in reporting to the General Assembly at New Haven in 1747 on the building's completion, called it "transcendently magnificent!". It was used continuously as a place of worship for seventy-two years, until the new building of 1819. The Episcopalians were also granted permission to use the building, which they did until land was given them in the corner of the burying ground for their new church of 1785.[12]

Men and women were seated separately in this, as in the former, meeting house, until either 1776 or 1783, when it was voted to seat men and women together "promiscuously". Seating in the church was still marked by social rank and prosperity (a prosperous man being a sign of a virtuous one in the eyes of God, although some who had dealings with Jabez Bacon (not a member of the church) and his relentless acquisition of worldly goods and canny profiteering, might have been justified in taking issue with that attitude). There was probably a gallery (or balcony) for servants, people of color (Native and African), and children to sit in. In the narthex of the current church, Lieutenant John Strong's pew remains. A small, simple seat, it has none of the grandeur or comfort of the present church, but attests to the strong, simple faith of that early stern Calvinist creed.

The second church had also a clock and a bell that was tolled at funerals and called members to worship. In those days with only the ambient noises of nature to interfere, the bell must have resounded throughout the valley. A reference to painting the building in 1789 suggests that it should "be near the color of Mr. Timothy Tomlinson except it be a little more of a greenish..." The bell was recast in 1790, possibly as the result of a windstorm damaging the steeple and bell. In 1794 an earlier vote to rebuild the steeple was revoked, probably because of the expense involved and the unwillingness of any individuals to shoulder that cost. The controversy over building a new church began at this point, signaling in earnest the start of the great split.[13]

---

[12] Saint Paul's Episcopal Church is the oldest church structure in Woodbury.

[13] Kelly, pg. 320

By the time of the controversy Woodbury had changed significantly as we have seen, and the town's stratified social structure had organized itself into four tiers, with a small class of wealthy leaders, a middling class of farmers, a class that provided non-agrarian services (Woodbury became a center for fine furniture making as well as general trade), and a class of landless agricultural laborers.[14]

As noted in the chapter on the great split, it is impossible to know what the members who chose to remain in the southern part of town were thinking, but the few references that come to us suggest that money was always an issue and probably becoming more of one as society moved farther away from the notion of Church and State being inseparable[15]. In the absence of a passion to move the church north, did the minority of men who resisted the change of site lack the means to move forcefully ahead on their own with a new building? Was it the goad of the lovely new church in North Woodbury (recognized almost as a new town of its own, with its own green and, later, post office) that finally moved those men to build the present church building? Or was it the resistance of the older, prominent men of property and status to guard their position in the town against the importuning of a younger generation of men that led them to build a larger, arguably more lovely, building? Was there a kind of class and generational conflict behind the new building? A more complete history of the town would have to answer those questions.

---

[14] Cooke., p. 14

[15] The Congregational Church and State were formally separated (disestablished) in 1818. Interestingly, the Episcopalians (Church of England) were arguably in the forefront of the notion of the desirability, for the health of religion, of the separation of Church and State. In 1783 a number of priests met in Woodbury, at the Glebe House, the Reverend John Marshall's home and farm, to elect one of their number (though he wasn't present) to seek the consecration of Bishop from the Church of England. The English not being interested, Seabury went to Scotland, where the Scottish Church, not part of the Scottish establishment, consecrated him, and the Episcopalians in America were no longer part of the established Church of England.

No matter the reasons, the third building of the First Congregational Church has proven itself over the centuries to be a lovely and commanding presence in the street-scape of Woodbury.

Coming from the south, the church spire becomes visible as one reaches the South Green. These days it doesn't command its site as North Church still does, but it is very much a presence on Main Street. Sited at the intersections of several roads that connect the center of town from its eastern and western sides to the north-south axis of Main Street, it seems to suggest that it is the true terminus of one's journey. Its lines are graceful, its size commanding, and it exudes a kind of self-assurance.

The building of the new church commenced in the spring of 1817. Harmon Stoddard drew up the plan for the new building on land that he owned. A note in the archives of the Old Woodbury Historical Society said to have been the recollection of William Forbes states that "Sheriff DeForest, by trade a mason, built the foundation of both Congregational churches and also built the Elizabeth Bull place, the Jabez Bacon and Nathan Warner houses of Judson Lane."[16] Who did the actual building of the church has, unfortunately, gone unremarked.

A vote to seat the meeting house was held in December, 1818, suggesting that the building was complete. This new building reflects the continuation of the transition of the buildings away from the meeting house plan and toward the church plan, and First Church represents a fine example of the church plan of building. The bell tower and steeple have been incorporated into the entry porch, rather than standing out in front of the building as the earlier building (and the 1785 St Paul's Church) had done. The church is on the west side of Main Street. The building is set back approximately 25 feet from the highway. Before paving and widening Main Street, the setback was probably greater, and the presentation of the

---

[16] "Incidents told or written by William Forbes and copied by Fannie Trowbridge and Lottie Hitchcock from his personal reminiscences. Nothing taken from Cothren", Woodbury Historical Society Archives, Churches Box 18

church more commanding. The main entrance, which faces eastward, is through this porch, with three doors representing the Holy Trinity, the middle door the largest of the three. Yale architecture professor Frederick Kelly writes that "The front entrance bay, while displaying great delicacy of scale in its details, exhibits the stilted "high-shouldered" proportions so often displayed by this feature of Connecticut meeting houses." [17] Kelly calls the steeple, "which consists of four stages, displays fine scale and harmonious proportions." Until the later 20th century, the steeple was embellished with Chippendale balustrades whose posts supported small turned urns. The gilded weather vane of a comet is still there and was a common embellishment, reflecting an actual celestial event. Frederick Kelly's description of the church is definitive, and he traces the changes to the building up until 1948 when his book was published.

Kelly notes changes to windows, walls and floors. He suggests that the galleries have been lowered, with changes to their supporting pillars and the cornice and paneled railing above them. There is a half-barrel vaulted ceiling, with the ceiling flat over the galleries themselves. More than almost any other feature, this high rounded ceiling that lifts the eye up toward the pulpit and its background reflects a differing approach to the religious experience in the building. While attention is drawn to the pulpit as in the past, the soaring nature of the ceiling high about suggests that the changing status of the minister, demoting him, in a sense, and raising awareness to God above all.

The pulpit itself also reflects changing attitudes. The original pulpit is gone, but probably was the high style of the day. In 1848 a vote was held to lower the pulpit "without expense to the Society," again suggesting the demotion of the minister. Apparently no one offered to actually pay for this, though, so it did not happen. Instead, the window in the wall behind the pulpit was closed in 1854 and the west wall behind it was furred out, leaving a large recess "back of the desk." $250 ($7,060 in 2019) was raised

---

[17] Kelly, 323.

to pay the Rev. R.S. Williams who built at his own expense the vestry room at the south side of the pulpit recess. At that time, according to the church records, seats were being sold for $500 ($14,119) annually. New seating, the bench pews that we enjoy today, were installed in 1855. Church records for 1855 noted that $3,005 ($83,520) had been subscribed for the alterations to the church. Charles A. Sumers was contracted for $3,450 ($93,916).[18]

1857 Pulpit

The current pulpit was installed in 1857 and reflects the mid 19th century esthetic of heavy and elaborate carving. It was installed by Derby Lumber and Building Co. November 1, 1857, with the carving done by J.T. Clinton, New Haven. Its elaborate nature of course reflects the fashions of the times, but it certainly it seems to upstage the minister who, one could argue, is diminished in stature by its bulk.

A furnace was installed in 1864. Before that there had been stoves which often were a source of controversy in churches all around New England,

---

[18] https://westegg.com/inflation/infl.cgi

with stories in many churches of women fainting after being overcome by the heat. For many of us now, that seems laughable when we struggle to get warm on a Sunday morning in the drafty auditorium of the church.

Additional repairs and changes were made. A new bell was installed in 1875. The pulpit was removed in 1881 and stored in the horse sheds behind the church; it was replaced in a major renovation and redecoration in 1928.

The Sanctuary in 1899. Note the pulpit and stenciling.

The chapel, or Parish House, was built in 1894. Funded by Mrs.Charlotte L.Lewis, whose picture graces the main reception room of the building, was until the 1980s a separate building with a dirt driveway between it and the church building. A portico was added between it and the vestry room door so that the minister and choir could pass between the buildings without being buffeted by inclement weather. The Sunday school was, at least in the 1950s and 60s, held in the basement. A dark space, with little windows high above the floor for minimal light, a typescript in the church records asserts that sometime in the 1940s of 50s an extensive rehabilitation of the Parish House basement (then a crawl space) was undertaken. Several of the active men of the church took part, including Heartt Raub whose account follows.

> What they did, in order to give space downstairs for church school classes, etc. was to go into the crawl space with picks and shovels and wheel barrows, and re-excavate the space to the depth where it would be possible to build usable space. The undertaking is not mentioned in any Annual Reports or Minutes of the church School Board that we can find. The people who remember it are uncertain of the exact date, and the men who did the work are no longer with us...[19]

Mr. & Mrs. J. Heartt Raub

---

[19] Sunday School typescript, author unknown, Church Archives

EXPANSION

In the early 1980's First Church brought to fruition an idea that had germinated for many years: expanding the church to provide for considerably more Sunday School space; purchasing the house next door and refurbishing it as a parsonage; and linking an expanded 1894 chapel with the main church. This required excavating beneath the parish house (chapel) to create six classrooms, additional meeting space, a church office, a storage area, and the minister's study. The parish house would be expanded by ten feet on the north side to link with the main body of the church.

Throughout the building project, First Church had to take especial care to conform the renovations to the church's architectural style and the town historic district. After the architect drew up the plans, they were submitted to Professor Vincent Scully, Chairman of the History of Art Department at Yale. Professor Scully was impressed by the design and its sensitivity to the architectural integrity of the existing structures. Fortunately, Professor Scully judged the plans to be "architecturally sympathetic to the history and quality of the existing buildings as well as to those of the newly acquired Terrill House on the south. I am reminded of the similar sympathetic development, especially in terms of roof profiles, of the Second Congregational Church of Hartford. In general.,the new grouping of buildings promises to be a very handsome one."[20]

To finance the project, the church first turned to its members, and the membership pledged to contribute $252,000, approximately 40% of the $650,000 needed to complete the project. Accordingly, the church turned to the wider community in early 1983 for help. In a letter sent to 400 community members, Harlan H. Griswold, Chairman of the Community Support program at the church and Chairman of the Connecticut

---

[20] Letter of Vincent Scully to Stedman Hitchcock, November 5, 1982. Archives of First Church. Mr. Hitchcock was Chairman of the Building Committee.

Historical Commission, outlined the church's need and asked them for pledges of $1000 each, payable over five years in installments of $200 each. ($1000 was actually considered a lot of money in those days.) Mr. Griswold also noted in the letter that of the 97 active families in the church six had pledged $5000 or more, eight had pledged at $3000 to $5000 and 25 pledged $1000 to $3000 for a three year period.[21]

Another part of the project involved selling the Noah B. Benedict parsonage located across Sycamore Avenue from the St. Paul's Episcopal Church and purchasing the Tony Pagano/Terrill house and butcher shop right next door. This involved ensuring that Benedict's gift of the parsonage through his will could be broken. Reflecting the old site controversy, Benedict wrote in his will that the parsonage was the church's as long as it did not move north from where it was currently located. The younger Benedict died in 1830. The controversy was still fresh a little over a decade past the new church building, but by the 1970s it was irrelevant. It made more sense for the minister and his family to live next door and the Pagano property's value for other purposes was sorely limited by its lack of acreage and its proximity to the church.

---

[21] Harlan H. Griswold, letter to prospective contributors in the archives of First Church. This letter is undated but is presumed to have been sent in early 1983 since the due date for receiving pledges was June, 1983.

Terrill House Parsonage

By the time the project was finished in 1984, the church had raised the necessary funds and realized what many had earnestly desired for years: viable meeting space; actual classrooms equipped for a modern Sunday school; and a handicapped-accessible facility.[22] Today, the rooms still fulfill their original purpose. The classrooms are occupied on Sunday by the Mattatuck Unitarian Universalist Sunday school. The Unitarian minister is accorded a study next to the pastor of First Church, and storage for the parish archives is provided.

---

[22] Members of the initial building committee were: Stedman Hitchcock, Chairman; Harlan Griswold; Helga Weed; Grace Limouze; Larae Graham; Earl Eyre; Eugene McKean; John Fleming; Rev. Russell Rowland; George Lewis; Charles Nininger; Norman Taylor.

The fact that the community as a whole stepped up to help this expansion underscores how much a part of the community First Church has always been. The church has reciprocated by making its space available for numerous town organizations and activities, opening its doors to AA groups, Scout groups, and many others, as well as offering community programs and events.

Again, as with the theology, Order of Worship, music performed by the choir and sung by the congregation, nothing in our beloved church building has been static. While its overarching use has continued to be as a sacred space, the ways in which that has been interpreted have changed as each generation has come along. At the same time, each generation has sustained this building "lovely in her bones" for the subsequent generations to come. With the development of the historic preservation movement in the 1960s and 70s, as a society we are more aware of how important it is to honor and sustain the presence of the past in our built landscapes. As we maintain our church building, we are honoring those ancestors who built it and used it to communicate who they were to both themselves and the community at large.

Church Interior

THE CHURCH SPLITS -
SURELY THE LORD IS IN THIS PLACE

A new Meeting House should be built on the West Side of the Highway, at the junction of the Middle Road Turnpike, Washington Turnpike, and the Litchfield County Road. [23]

The decision to build two Congregational churches in Woodbury less than a mile apart from one another has vexed both churches for 200 years. Efforts to reunite the two churches have been broached for at least 100 years, most recently in the 2010s, but to no avail, though relations between the two churches remain cordial.

In the appeal of 1816, petitioners claimed that there had been forty years of dissension over the matter of the placement of the new church building; meaning that since 1776 there had been debate about the siting of a new church. Perhaps it was inevitable that an organization born of dissension would have some kind of propensity for it encoded in its organizational DNA.

Although the name of the new church, The Strict Congregational Society, suggested that there were doctrinal issues that separated it from the First Ecclesiastical Society, in fact, the petitions to the Connecticut Assembly reference the conflict over siting the church and not differences in theology. Calling North Church the Strict Congregational Society

---

[23] Cothren, Vol. I, 310, 1814

seems to have been almost entirely a matter of expediency, since the General Assembly would not countenance two Congregational societies with similar theologies so close together.

At this remove, it is hard to understand why the location of a church building would matter so much that the Society would be riven and the Congregational Church in Woodbury ultimately weakened by being divided, but a review of the circumstances of the time may shed some light on what to us just looks like the cranky, Yankee stubbornness.

The story of Woodbury's initial settlement has been well described in William Cothren's History of Ancient Woodbury. Originally encompassing what are now the towns of Southbury, Roxbury, Washington, and Bethlehem (along with some territory annexed to Middlebury and Oxford), the siting of the original meeting house was more or less centrally located, following the plans of Colonial towns. "In most towns it [the meetinghouse] occupied the central site, and its early erection was a matter of pride. Within its walls not only Sunday worship but also much town business was conducted." [24] In addition to the practical matter of providing a relatively easily reached place for a dispersed population to gather, the location of the meetinghouse reflected the complete integration of spiritual and civic life in the early town and the significance of the place also reflected its moral and ethical, as well as its legal power. [25]

The original town encompassed the Pomperaug River watershed area, itself a part of the Housatonic River watershed and a unique part of the western uplands of Connecticut in that it is a small rift valley with rich alluvial soils in its center valley allowing for tillage and pasture land with its natural meadow and silt lands with few rocks and stones.[26] The early

---

[24] Garvan, 32.

[25] "The often repeated truism that a the meetinghouse was after all not a church and was habitually used was civil meeting place obscures the very real veneration in which the town held it." *Ibid*,143.

[26] *Ibid*,. 14-15.

Anglo families who arrived here found the valley already cleared and cultivated by the local indigenous people and it made perfect sense for them to settle along the valley, creating a town center that followed the Native people's trail.

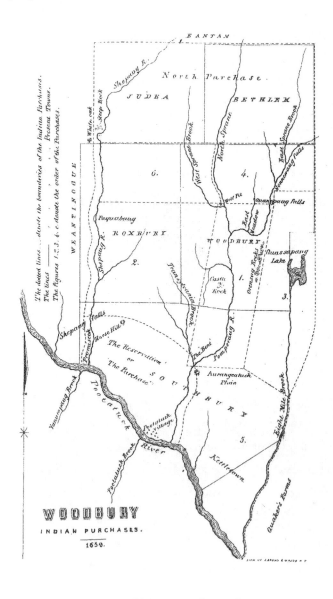

Original Territory of Woodbury

Their meeting house occupied the approximate center of the large community which stretched from the confluence of the Housatonic River and Eight Mile Brook in the south, to just west of the Shepaug River in the west, the boundary with Bantam in the north, and just east of Lake Quassapaug in the east. By the time of the Revolutionary War, the town had grown to about 5,000 inhabitants and was according to the 1776 tax returns, the fourth wealthiest town in the State, beating out Stratford, Fairfield, and Hartford. [27]

However, as the population grew and spread throughout the territory, families living in the outlying areas requested and were granted permission to create parishes with their own ministers and meeting houses. By the end of the 18th century, these had become incorporated towns.[28] Woodbury thus had lost much of its land and diminished to a population of 1,944. However, in spite of these losses, Woodbury continued to prosper, having retained the best farmland and continuing to be the market town for the area.[29]

Woodbury's situation in the early 19th century was not dissimilar from other growing communities in Connecticut. As Anthony Garvan writes:

Such extensive first settlement resulted not in a series of well-integrated although separate towns splitting off

---

[27] Jane Platt Sturges and Susan J. Shepard, American Revolution Bicentennial 1776 Woodbury 1976 (Woodbury Bicentennial Committee, 1976)

[28] The members of First Congregational Church appear not to have been entirely happy about this: in October, 1786, the Church meeting voted to "appoint an Agent to attend the General Assembly this instant to remonstrate against the two petitions…to divide Bethlem *(sic)* from the rest of the town and incorporate them into a town and also Southbury & South Britain (those parishes had already been established). "Copy of the Records of the First Ecclesiastical Society of the First Congregational church in Woodbury, Connecticut December 17, 1770 - June1, 1854 Volume One" Typescript in First Church Archive

[29] A Historic and Architectural Resource Survey in the Town of Woodbury, Vol.I (Cunningham & Associates, Ltd.. Middletown, CT, 1991-92), 15

from the parent town over a period of years but in a single discordant unit which spread over all the township's land. Congregations disputed endlessly over the choice of a minister or the location of the meetinghouse, and even after a vote minorities seldom abandoned their stand. Without stores, harbors, or main roads the location of the town's center became a devious religious question upon the solution of which each settler's attendance on the Sabbath depended. As town grew, only direct, divine intervention could have kept the town's population center near its meetinghouse site, and this seldom happened. "[30]

In October of 1816, 102 people (of which *(sic)* five were women) signed a petition to the General Assembly of Connecticut to "incorporate them and their associates into an ecclesiastical society: by the name of the Strict Congregational Society in Woodbury..." [31] This petition references forty years of dissension over the siting of a new meeting house. It also references "several" meetings in 1795 to discuss the siting of the new building, and states that "a large majority" were in favor of siting the building in the center of the Society, but two thirds of the legal votes in the Society did not concur.

What were "legal votes"? The answer to that question goes back to the history of the Congregational Church in its earliest days. Originally, the people who eventually became known as Congregationalists, did not want to abolish the Anglican creed, but objected to the Anglican Church governance structure and hierarchy, believing them to have become irredeemably corrupt. Accordingly, in creating new churches, "they declared that the final authority in all church affairs should be the autonomous and independent single congregations."[32] Although the General Court (in

---

[30] Garvan, p. 63

[31] Charlotte H. Isham, Arthur N. Johnson, Frederick T. Strong, <u>One Hundred Fifty Years in an Old Parish</u>,1966.

[32] Marion Mabey, <u>First Congregational Church Woodbury, Connecticut</u>, 1994, 2.

Connecticut at this time Church and State were, more or less, one) could advise, it could not overrule decisions made by the congregation as a whole. In addition, the early churches restricted membership in an attempt to avoid the laxity of the Anglican Church and maintain the purity of belief. Therefore, only full church members held the legal vote. As Mabey points out "partial members...would have no vote in church affairs and could not partake of the Lord's Supper." [33] Although by the time of the vote of 1795 criteria for church membership had loosened with a new covenant, there was apparently still a legal division in First Church. Therefore, the 1816 petition states that in 1795 there were about 130 legal voters in the Society. Women did not have the vote, of course, no matter what their status as members, and there were probably others who didn't qualify to vote, which would put the church body as a whole at about close to 300. In other words, about 85 people brought the whole decision about where to site the church to a standstill. After 40 years, two generations, the lines were still drawn and the impasse continued unabated.

In 1813 a new site had been designated 120 rods north of the second meeting house, or less than half a mile north of its existing position near the current intersection of Hollow Road and Main Street. That building was never built, probably in part because it wouldn't have brought the church significantly nearer to the northern part of town. No doubt fed up with the impasse, and perhaps assuming that it would be easier to get permission if they already had a building, 102 petitioners to the Connecticut General Assembly stated that they had gone ahead and built themselves a new church near the site designated in 1795 and asked the General Assembly to grant them a charter, which was done. This new church was called "The Strict Congregational Society" and the bill passed on October 2, 1816, effectively creating two congregational churches with the same "limits and boundaries" as the First Ecclesiastical Society.

---

[33] *Ibid*, 3.

Missionary Work

Throughout the Nineteenth Century, and well into the Twentieth, First Church was especially active in providing young missionaries committed to spreading the Gospel and providing financial support to their efforts. This was in accordance with the missionary efforts of New England Congregational churches, which began during the Second Great Awakening, sparked by a tumultuous revival meeting at Cane Ridge, Kentucky, in 1800. At the time, strongly religious people shared an acute and alarming awareness that the beliefs of most Americans had traveled to Unitarianism or Deism. Jefferson himself predicted, at the outset of the Nineteenth Century, that most Americans would die as Unitarians or Deists. With highly-emotional camp meetings and an exuberant approach to worship, Methodists brought Christianity to the frontier early on through their circuit riders, so that by 1840 Methodists could claim to be the largest Christian denomination in the United States. The Baptists, for their part, followed the Methodists and quickly outshone them; by 1860 Baptists surpassed the Methodists as the largest Christian denomination.

New England Congregationalists were comparatively slow to respond to the missionary need on the American frontier. As one observer put it, "The Methodists came on horseback. The Baptists came by carriage. The Presbyterians came by stagecoach, and the Episcopalians came by Pullman car." Usually, the Congregationalist clergy were largely uninterested in winning converts on the frontier with wild tent meetings and highly emotional revivals; instead they preferred to follow New England settlements across the upper Northwest, following the trail of settlement to the Oregon territory.[34]

But if New England Congregationalists showed themselves reluctant to evangelize the frontier, they showed no such hesitation about venturing to foreign lands, forming the American Board of Commissioners for Foreign Missions in 1810 and working cooperatively with the Presbyterians. Setting its sights first on Hawaii (the Sandwich Islands), a group of twenty-three young missionaries set sail from Boston on October 23, 1819, and established missions, schools, medical facilities, and other institutions there. Although portrayed somewhat infamously by James Michener's novel Hawaii, the missionaries accomplished considerable progress in advancing literacy and health. They even established a school for Hawaiians in Cornwall, Connecticut, which functioned briefly until the local farmers complained about the students, who proved attractive to their daughters.[35] According to the instructions of the Reverend Samuel Worcester, secretary of the Board of Missions, to the missionaries,

'You are to aim at nothing short of covering those islands with fruitful fields and pleasant dwellings and schools and churches; of raising up the whole people to an elevated state of Christian civilization; of bringing, or preparing the means of bringing, thousands and millions of the present and succeeding generations to the mansions of blessedness." [36]

All told, the Board of Commissioners sent out 147 ordained men to many lands and had multiple missionary stations on every continent by 1855. First Church proved a fount of Christian spirituality throughout the Nineteenth Century and sent its share of missionaries to foreign lands.

---

[34] Sidney Ahlstrom, A Religious History of the American People (New Haven: Yale University Press, 1976) *passim.*

[35] John P. Demos, The Heathen School: A Story of Hope and Betrayal in the Age of the Early Republic New York: Vintage Books, 2014), 129-195.

[36] Dudley Pratt, "Go Ye Therefore and Teach All nations" in "Parnelly Pierce Andrews" Archives of the First Congregational Church, Woodbury, CT

Woodbury contributed its young women especially to the foreign missions. Perhaps the first notable woman to take an active role in the Hawaiian missions was Parnelly Pierce Andrews, born in Woodbury in 1807. A devoutly religious young girl, she owned the First Church Covenant in January, 1822, and set upon a career in teaching. After the death of her parents in 1835-1836, she determined to spread the Gospel as a missionary.[37] This opportunity came when she married Doctor Seth L. Andrews of Putney, Vermont, who took her to Hawaii as part of his medical mission there. According to a contemporary account, Dr. Andrews' time was stretched among the six medical stations operated by the Missionary Board in the islands. When he traveled, his wife "performed his duties as a physician, and manifested much judgment and skill in the healing art."[38] In a letter to Miss Anne A. Andrews of Pittsford, New York, dated December 3, 1837, she writes, "I have had occasion to remove several tumors, most marvelous stories have gone abroad respecting them. One of them was large about 10 in. in circumference, taken from the back part of a man's head. I have it in a jar standing upon my shelf, and it often brings me a crowd of visitors."[39]

When unburdened with her medical work, Parnelly supervised and taught in two schools, each with about 300 students.

With her long hours of work and frequent bouts of illness it is not surprising that life in Hawaii proved insurmountable for Parnelly Pierce Andrews. She bore three children there; three of her four children, Elizabeth, Lucy, and Charles, died in early infancy in Hawaii. In a letter

---

[37] Rev. Stuart Brush, "Foreword" in *Ibid*. (pages unnumbered)

[38] "Biographical Notice of Mrs. Andrews" The Friend (September, 1846, pages unnumbered) in ibid. The Friend was a missionary newspaper that covered events in the missions of Hawaii. It began publication in 1845 and ceased in 1902.

[39] Letter of Seth Land Parnelly Pierce Andrews to Miss Anne A. Andrews, Pittsford, New York, December 3, 1837. Reprinted in "Parnelly Pierce Andrews" Archives of the First Congregational Church, Woodbury.

to the Rev. Eleazar True of Pittsford New York, dated September 6, 1842, she writes:

> Our Father in heaven saw it to be best for His and His own glory & in an unexpected manner took to himself a treasure which but a few months previously he had committed to us. Our dear Elizabeth Woodbury was laid from her Mother's arms to an early grave, but it is allright. Tho' she will not return to us we shall go to her, & we trust that this sore bereavement will the better prepare us for our own departure.

The letters she wrote to other missionaries detail the physical travails of life in that distant land; she, her husband, and the children were afflicted with long bouts of dysentery several times every year. One imagines that their digestive systems were infected by local bacteria to which New Englanders had no immunities. All of her surviving letters express concern for the addressee's health and a discussion of the family's many physical afflictions. Many of the missionaries to whom she wrote lost young children. And death was never far off on her horizon. She herself died of dysentery on September 29, 1846, within a few months of giving birth to her last child, Charles, who followed her in death a short time later. Parnelly was buried in the churchyard of Mokuaikaua Church, Kailua-Kona. Her husband Seth returned to the United States, ultimately remarried, and died in 1892. George, their only child to survive early childhood, died in 1903.

What truly awakened many New England Congregationalists to the need for missionaries in the United States, but outside the northwestern areas where New Englanders settled, was the need of education for newly-freed blacks in the South after the Civil War. Abolitionists formed the American Missionary Association as early as 1840 with the goal of evangelizing blacks, but the era of Reconstruction in the South presented a significant opportunity to accomplish that mission through education. Toward these efforts, the young people of First Church contributed in a major way with financial support from both the parish and the A.M.A. A pamphlet published by the Mission Circle of First Church in 1922 provided a list of these missionaries, who worked in schools under the auspices of the Freedman's Bureau in Washington.

As excerpt from that pamphlet follows:

"Mrs. Sarah (Barnes) Rathburn, one of the earliest volunteers to teach among the colored people of the south at Vicksburg and Galveston.

Mrs. Eliza (Summers) Hitchcock who was sent by the A.M.A. to Hilton head, South Carolina, in January, 1867.

Mrs. Julia (Benedict) Smith, who served with Mrs. Hitchcock at Hilton Head island and in Camp Distribution in Virginia among the colored children, and again in Fiske University, Nashville, Tenn. From 1869 to 1871.

Mrs. Carolina (Curtiss) White, sent under the A.M.A. to Hampton, Virginia in 18678

Miss Hattie Judson, who accompanied Mrs. White in 1867 and served several years.

Rev. R.A. Fowles, who served under the A.M.A. as principal of Grandview Normal School, Grandview, Tennessee, 1912 to 1915."[40]

Very little information is available about any of these missionaries except Sarah Barnes Rathburn. Born in 1838 and nurtured in the Christian faith at First Church, Sarah trained to be a teacher and, at the age of twenty-six, set out to teach black people in the South. Under the auspices of the American Missionary Association she went south to Union occupied areas in 1864. For a while she taught black children at Davis bend, where

---

[40] "Souvenir: Fortieth Anniversary of the Founding of The Mission Circle of First Congregational Church, Woodbury, Conn" Archives of the First Congregational Church, Woodbury.

she lived at a plantation owned by Jefferson Davis but occupied by Federal troops. The writer Janet Sharp Herman wrote of the experiences of young women on the Davis plantation:

> What sort of people were these emissaries from the North who formed the new white elite at Davis bend? The majority of them were young women from middle class families who came South with a sincere desire to help the poor victims of slavery. The conditions under which they had to live must have tested their enthusiastic commitment. The only housing available was in the deserted mansions, which had been stripped of furniture and were in sad disrepair. On the Davis plantation the teachers were housed in the Brierfield mansion, where souvenir hunters had removed even the door locks and the marble mantels. Although the missionaries brought a few items of furniture there were few comforts. Besides fostering disease, the hot, humid summers must have made life difficult for these newcomers. In May Lieutenant Barnes (no relation to Sarah) reported 'the gnats are biting terribly and it is almost impossible to write at all.' Horses, mules, or any other forms of conveyance were scarce here, so teachers often walked several miles to their schoolrooms on dusty roads under a scorching sun in summer, or through ankle-deep mud in freezing rain in the winter.[41]

Sometime later, Sarah Barnes moved to Galveston, Texas, with another A.M.A. missionary, and was promptly dispatched by the Texas

---

[41] Janet Sharp Hermann, 'The Pursuit of a Dream' quoted in James W. Hosking, "Sarah Maria Barnes Rathburn"p.1., this is a manuscript in the archives of the First Congregational Church.

reconstruction government to the little village of Magoffinsville, near the Rio Grande. Apparently she stayed only briefly at Magoffinsville, for she left within a year to return to Galveston and founded the Barnes Institute with fellow-teacher Sarah Skinner. But she soon found that students did not automatically show up; the pair of teachers had to visit local homes to recruit students. According to Sarah Barnes' diary for March 14, 1868, "Two of the children of the first house we entered we found were attending our day school and we were greeted by the parents. They seemed perfectly delighted because 'the school mistis" had come. We introduced our Bible Class which they had already heard about from someone attending and who reported to them 'they never heard so such structions 'fore, and by way of compliment to us added "we is mighty proud we goes.' At another home she visited the mother voiced some suspicion but said she would do anything 'fo de Yankees' and she 'sposed you is dey.'[42]

While at Galveston, Sarah Barnes met sea Captain Nathan Warren Rathbun, whom she married in his home town of Noank, Connecticut, in 1870. For the rest of her husband's life Sarah Rathbun traveled on his voyages all over the world, and her diary contains many descriptions of places as Far Tortuga, Malta, and Constantinople. Nevertheless, she kept up correspondence with former teachers and students. Her school, the Barnes institute was absorbed into the Galveston public school system. After Rathbun's death in 1879, she moved to Danbury, where she operated a millenary ship. The end of her life found her at Woodbury, where she suffered from the tuberculosis that she had contracted in Mississippi. She died in Woodbury on November 17, 1886[43]

As one reads these names today it is easy to forget just how dangerous this work was. The Ku Klux Klan, founded in 1868 by former Confederate General Nathan Bedford Forrest to violently oppose the Reconstruction governments and their institutions, posed a daily threat to the lives of

---

[42] *Ibid.*, 3.

[43] *Ibid.*, 13.

these young women. While the Klan generally contented themselves with killing Republican officeholders and the blacks who supported them, many schools were torched by the Klan or similar white supremacist organizations, and they used every opportunity to intimidate these strong willed young teachers to "go back to where you came from." Although the noble experiment in Reconstruction ended with the Compromise of 1877, when President Hayes withdrew federal troops protecting Republican governments in the South, many of the educational institutions that the New Englanders founded endured.[44] These institutions taught blacks to become school teachers and trained a whole generation of blacks to staff the segregated schools of the South. Fisk University has stood for many years as a premier black university, and it remained so even after its incorporation into Vanderbilt University. Howard University, founded by the A.M.A., stands today as the premier black university in the United States.

The late Nineteenth Century brought renewed interest in missionary activity both in New England as a whole and in the little town of Woodbury. Queen Victoria's proclamation of the British Empire in 1873 inaugurated this new era of missionary work from the Anglo-Saxon world. This time, missionaries followed soldiers, and wherever the British and American empires spread, Protestant missionaries converted and educated large numbers in Christianity and European ways. First Church women organized to support these missionary efforts when they formed a Mission Circle in 1881. Fortunately for us living in the present, the reports of the Mission Circle are preserved in the Church Records of the early Twentieth Century[45] The Circle sponsored many find-raising events over the years, an example of which is the "Eight-Cent Sale on August 8, 1922. For the

---

[44] Eric Foner, <u>Reconstruction: America's Unfinished Revolution, 1863-1877</u> (New York: Harper & Row, 1988), 144-147.

[45] "Records of the First Congregational Church, Woodbury, Connecticut" 1921-1948. These are archived at the Woodbury Church and at the Connecticut State Library in Hartford.

admission price of eight cents, one would be admitted to the town hall, where all hand-crafted items would cost only eight cents. Why they chose eight cents is a mystery today, but one imagines thrifty Yankees not being able to pass it up.[46]

BUTTERFLY FETE!

The Young Ladies' Mission Circle of the First Congregational Church, Woodbury, will celebrate their tenth anniversary by holding a "Butterfly Fete" on the

PARKER HOUSE LAWN,
THURSDAY EVENING,
AUG. 15, '95,
BEGINNING AT 6 O'CLOCK.

Among the attractions will be
FANCY ARTICLES, BUTTERFLIES,
Ice Cream, Cake, Home-made Candy and Lemonade.

The Woodbury Reporter Book and Job Print, Woodbury.

Flyer for Fundraiser

At the meeting in January, 1922, Mrs. George Starr presented the annual report for 1921. She made note of a missionary from First Church

---

[46] "Souvenir: Fortieth Anniversary of the Founding of the Mission Circle of the First Congregational Church, Woodbury, Conn." A pamphlet published by the Mission Circle in 1922, in the archives of the First Congregational Church.

to India, the late Mrs. Minnie Sibley, who had spoken to the church on the previous April 23 of her mission work, but who drowned on her way back to India. Mrs. Starr commented that,… "we cannot yet understand why after forty years of service there why she should have drowned on her way back for further service. But her sweet and earnest personality still blesses us."[47] In that same report, Mrs. Starr noted the June 11th address of "our own missionary" Miss Minnie Carter, who spoke about missionary work in among the Zulus in South Africa.[48] Mrs. Julia Minor Strong presented the highlight of the evening, a biographical sketch of her sister, Miss Emily Minor, active in the mission field in India. She was born in Waterbury, but after the death of her parents, she moved to her sister Julia's home in Woodbury. A graduate of Mount Holyoke Seminary, Emily Minor taught in area schools until she felt a call to missionary work. Sometime in the 1880s she left Woodbury to work at the DeWitt Memorial Church on Rivington Street in New York City, ministering among the immigrant population. In September, 1891, she left for India, to work in a large city, Ratuagiri, about twenty-five miles south of Bombay. In the large American settlement there, which featured a hospital, a dispensary, a leper asylum, and an orphanage as well as schools, Emily Minor taught from second grade to high school. She also worked heavily in evangelization, translating books of the Bible into the local Marathi dialect for use in Bible classes. Her sister commented that Miss Minor had made three return trips to America and always spent time among the people of Woodbury.[49]

The Mission Circle existed until 1940, when several ladies groups consolidated into one and the missionary impulse was largely lost. Not only did World War II, which broke out in 1939, make missionary work highly perilous, but the need for women volunteers to support the War effort also undermined missionary activity by channeling the women's

---

[47] "Records," 15.

[48] *Ibid.*

[49] *Ibid.*, 16.

efforts into a new, all-consuming cause. But it should not be forgotten that, for well over a century, First Church supplied and financially supported both domestic and foreign missionaries, often brave young women who undertook the missions at their own physical peril, at great distances from their homes and families. They learned the Christian faith at First Church, and they carried it throughout the world.

OUTREACH

The Elderly Housing Initiative

Although First Church stopped supporting missionary work, its outreach efforts continued without a break in other ways. Contributions to UCC mission efforts and local outreach have always been a significant part of First Church life.

In the 1970's more and more Woodburians talked about providing affordable elderly housing for the town's residents. As a fast-growing town in the 1970's and 1980's, Woodbury saw its taxes jump as roads, schools, and other town services expanded and required increased funding. This put many of the town's elderly homeowners in a perilous financial position. Often, life-long residents living on fixed incomes could not afford to stay in town, but had to sell their homes and down-size, often in other places.

In the spring of 1978, then, First Church took the lead in proposing the idea of forming a committee to support the construction of elderly housing in town. Members of the congregation held a special meeting after morning worship on March 25, 1978, and unanimously endorsed a series of resolutions that supported the concept of "church related organizations using government funding implemented by the Good Samaritan Housing Corporation."[50] This corporation was an arm of the Connecticut Conference of the United Church of Christ. The resolutions

---

[50] Minutes of meeting of March 25, 1987 held in the archives of First Church in the folder "Elderly Housing."

further authorized the church to appoint the first three members of an Interim Committee to interface with Good Samaritan and appropriated $2,500 as "seed money" to begin the process.

A formidable leader in the effort was Stedman Hitchcock. According to Larae Graham, Hitchcock was a powerful, albeit quiet, leader in both town and First Church. "If he said it, it was done…you really didn't question any of his decisions, you just went along."[51] Apparently, Mr. Hitchcock owned the property and conveyed it to the town at a very reasonable price.

Mr. Stedman Hitchcock

Rev. Mr. William Inderstrodt, chair of Good Samaritan, came to Woodbury in December, 1978, to discuss plans with the newly formed

---

[51] Interview with Larae Graham by Sarah Griswold, October 11, 2019, in the archives of First Church.

committee, the town selectmen, and the Commission on the Elderly. By now the committee included representatives from North Congregational, First Methodist, St. Paul's Episcopal, and St. Theresa's Roman Catholic churches. Since New Samaritan had been involved in building several other housing projects for the elderly in other towns, the town and church leadership rapidly endorsed the plans and moved forward. By February, 1979, the Elderly Commission had approved the plans and recommended them to the Board of Selectmen.[52]

Once zoning issues were resolved, the plans moved quickly. By January, 1980, Dr. Theodore Martland reported to the Elderly Commission that he hoped to have 20 housing units ready by January, 1981. The Committee still had obstacles to surmount: the Federal Housing Administration required that the rooms be smaller, and The Connecticut Commission on Human Rights and Opportunities required that the housing be open to all Connecticut residents because of the lack of racial minorities in Woodbury.[53]

The housing opened close to schedule, with 14 initial units, which have been added to over time. Today, seniors in the Woodbury apply for apartments well in advance. They must meet income-means criteria, which change modestly through the years. This project remains neat, clean, and well-maintained. Indeed it has been a godsend to elders in need of downsizing, but who wish to remain in town.

---

[52] "Elderly Housing Approved, <u>Voices</u>, Feb. 7, 1979, p.3. This clipping is filed in the archives of First Church in the folder "Elderly Housing." Among those First Church members who served on the Committee were: Theodore Burghart, Chairman; Montgomery Woolson; Lois Tuley; Roger Turrill; Ruth Baggs; Irene Boultbee; Stedman Hithcock.

[53] "Senior Housing Due to Open in January" <u>Voices</u>, Nov. 7, 1979, p. 33. This clipping is filed in the archives of First Church in the "Elderly Housing" folder.

The Living Creche

In the early 1980s, First Church for several years held a "Living Creche" at first on the church lawn and later down the street. Church members dressed as figures at the crèche and local people lent use of their animals for the evening. The community was invited to join in the Christmas caroling which went on around the crèche. the Choir of First Church providing a nucleus of strong singers, many community members from the other churches (and perhaps no church at all) joined in this community celebration of the birth of Christ. Why it was not continued remains a mystery, although one can imagine the logistics of assembling the crèche, rounding up and transporting the animals and keeping them under control must have been wearying after a few years. The humans were probably the least of the problem.[54]

---

[54] Interview with William Geddes, prominent music teacher and tireless promoter of music in Woodbury, December 13, 2019.

Living Creche, ca. 2000

The Red Barn and Parsonage Boutique

Red Barn with managers Mary McLeod and Virginia
Garms, 2020. Photo credit S. Griswold

According to the recollections of Larae Graham, the Red Barn opened as a thrift shop in about 1993. Until then, the barn was used as a place where "they let the teenagers go over there and use as a spot where they didn't have to behave themselves."[55] According to Mrs. Graham, "I was at a council meeting and we were discussing what to do with it and I suggested we turn it into a thrift shop. And they said, well you want to go ahead and do a little planning on it? And I did. It started off as a committee run enterprise: Connie O'Brien, because she was he guru of thrift shops and

---

[55] Interview with Larae Graham by Sarah Griswold, October 11, 2019, stored in the archives of First Church.

consignment shops; Grace Limouze because she had loads of experience at Southbury Training School; Jane Sturges because Jane had good taste and at the same time was practical; Lois Cameron, she was interested in details and liked to fix things. Those are the only ones I can think of at the moment. Eleanor Monckton came on and she offered to be chairman of the whole thing. So I was off. Later I was back and helping. It was really an immediate hit."[56] Over the years, the Red barn has provided hundreds of thousands of dollars worth of high-quality clothing to the community. Mary MacLeod stated that the Red Barn aims to achieve $40,000 in sales per year and the actual figures have ranged between $34,000 in a lean year to $56,000 in a good year. The products that are left unsold are then sold to A&E Clothing, a textile recycling plant in New Jersey, which keeps the fabrics out of the landfills. Last year (2018), the Red Barn sold over four tons of unsold clothing to the recycling company.[57]

Each year, the Red Barn has to make do with fewer volunteers; twenty years ago, there were eighteen volunteers, but in 2019 there are four volunteers willing to work the full day (10 a.m. to 3 p.m.) and five volunteers able to work a half-day. The diminution in volunteers is attributable to three factors: many "aged out" and are now caring for parents and grandchildren; a fair number have died, and many young women are out in the workplace today.[58]

Many have questioned what will become of the Red barn now that the future of the church is uncertain. Larae, Mary, and others hope that a way can be found to preserve this important outreach to the town. Mary MacLeod stated, "We did the best we could with what we had."[59] And that achievement is no small matter.

---

[56] *Ibid.*

[57] Interview with Mary MacLeod, December 6, 2019.

[58] *Ibid.*

[59] *Ibid.*

Youth Mission Trips

In July, 1998, members of the church Pilgrim Fellowship traveled to Birmingham, Alabama, under the leadership of Pastor Mark Heilshorn, to rebuild an African-American church that had been destroyed in a fire. Although the church was not burned by arsonists, but was collateral damage from a fire in a house next door, the local young people eagerly undertook the mission for a congregation that lacked the financial resources to rebuild. The previous year, pastor mark had let the young people to Greensboro, North Carolina to rebuild a church there. According to an account in Voices "The group worked hard, slept in a gymnasium, and put up with temperatures of 105 degrees. Yet...they talked not about how hard it was but what they had gained from the experience, the fun they had together, and how beneficial it was to each of them."[60]

The following year, in the summer of 1999, Pastor Heilshorn led the young people to Buffalo, South Carolina to help rebuild Rice Chapel A.M.E. Zion Church, which had burned in 1994. The young people took a 15-passenger van, and led by Mr. Heilshorn and Jeff Garms, they spent weeks applying spackle, sanding, and painting. One student remarked that the experience "improved my relationship with God and with other people too. I made a lot of friends while we were there."[61] Additional mission trips took the youth on trips from Maine to the Gulf Coast and helped First Church to better understand the needs of the wider world. The young people put into practice what the early Church fathers called "the liturgy

---

[60] Amy Capossela, "Parishioners Help Rebuild Church" Voices July 15, 1998, 16. In archives of the First Church.mMembers of the group were Mark Heilshorn; Chris Jensen; Erica Cooper; Marcia Pattillo-Crowe; Ryan Murphy; Doug England; Emily Munson; Matthew Jensen; John Craft; Maggie Pattillo and Claire Froggatt.

[61] Jean Dunn, "Confirmation Class Works on Church," in Voices, Aug. 4, 1999, 31. In archives of First Church. Members of that Confirmation class were: Matt Cole; Steven Kenny; Andrew Euston; Mike Crutchfield and Amy Soderberg.

after the liturgy," the extension of one's Christian values beyond the walls of the church building to the world.

Mission Trip, ca. 2000s. From Left Kyle Robinson, Matthew Crutchfield, Meredith Sherwood

Sharing our Facilities

In 2015, members of First Church and the Mattatuck Unitarian-Universalist Society initiated discussion of how the two churches might share the facilities at First Church. The Mattatuck Unitarian-Universalist society was a relatively new congregation in Woodbury, being only thirty-seven years old, and had rented space in a Pomperaug Road facility in Southbury for several years.

Unitarianism itself largely evolved out of Congregationalism in Massachusetts in the 19th Century, although the first officially Unitarian church in the United States was an Anglican congregation, King's Chapel in Boston. In the late 18th Century the Enlightenment spirit spread in the new

United States as the new nation reflected the political and philosophical principles of the English Enlightenment. Many Congregationalist clergy had doubts about the Trinity and had, in effect, adopted a theology similar to the Third Century Arians. They believed that Jesus was God's son and specially favored by God, but was not his equal.[62] Especially after the ordination of Jared Sparks by William Ellery Channing in 1816, Unitarianism openly broke with Congregationalism. Most Congregational churches in eastern Massachusetts voted to affiliate with the Unitarian movement, and the Trinitarians formed their own churches in response.[63]

Over time, Unitarianism developed a wide diversity of belief in its ranks, and Unitarians united with the Universalists, a sect formed in the 19th Century teaching universal salvation. Today, some Unitarian-Universalist congregations claim the label "Christian," and have a liturgy virtually indistinguishable from that of Congregational Churches, but most do not, preferring not to adhere to any creed, and designating themselves a "post-Christian" denomination.

---

[62] The Council of Nicea, which formulated the Nicene Creed in 325 C.E., defined Jesus as of the same substance (homoousios) as God and not merely of similar substance (homoiousios) as the Arians taught.

[63] Park Street Church in Boston was formed specifically to combat the Unitarianism of the Arlington Street Church directly across the Boston Common. Rev, Lyman Beecher left his pastorate in Litchfield and his position as chair of the Litchfield South Association to pastor the Park Street Church.

MUSIC AT FIRST CHURCH

Music is an integral part of the worship service and the community-building that is at the heart of First Church. As with so much of the history of First Church, its musical life follows the development of the larger culture's understanding of the importance and proper form music should take in religious life.

In his comprehensive history "America's Musical Life", Richard Crawford points out that sacred music reflects "fundamental ideas of the religious outlook it represents." He notes that Protestant music "may be seen as a critique of music of the Roman Catholic Church."[64] Music in the Catholic liturgy was seen as a tool that could bring people to a sense of piety and was directed through the senses. The music was a manifestation from above of the Divine, and the music produced was composed, orchestrated, and performed carefully. The Calvinists who inspired Congregationalism, on the other hand, believed in the power of individuals and their congregational associations to decide matters for themselves and to have a direct, unmediated experience of God without the interventions of priests, hierarchy, or rituals. This meant that parishioners were encouraged to become literate so they could read scripture for themselves. As the Word was the preeminent means of access to the divine, other forms were suspect, including music. As Crawford points out, Calvin and his followers rejected the idea that musical skill was worth cultivating

---

[64] Richard Crawford, America's Musical Life (New York: Norton, 2001), 31

in God's service, though singing was very much a part of worship. The Puritans "objected to the use of musical instruments in churches as well as an to an elaborate vocal liturgy, because they associated these with the "Romish" ritual that they strongly repudiated."[65] This resulted in a form of singing without any instruments, parts, or texts other than the Psalms. [66] Only a pitch pipe was used. The musical style that was preferred was a kind of "contrary plainness". This form of music making was referred to as "The Old Way", and reformers starting in the 18th century described it as a cacophony, although as we shall see, they had an ax to grind with this form of music making, and though not refined, it had its own internal structure. The main feature of this type of music was that each individual gave voice in his or her own way, as befit a spiritual practice that sought the individual's direct, personal experience of the Divine.

One of the ways of singing that was adopted to assist the illiterate or those without psalm books to refer to is called "Lining Out". In this form of singing a leader sings first, and the congregation follows. John Cotton describes this in 1647 as "it will be a necessary help, that the words of the Psalme be openly read before hand, line after line, or two lines together, that so they who want (or lack) either books or skill to read, may know what is to be sung, and join with the rest in the cutie of singing."[67] Although widespread, this practice was not universal and depended at least in part on the literacy of the congregation. It is unknown to what extent the singers of First Church relied on lining out; the records are silent on the matter. In writing about Scottish singing, Gilbert Chase suggests that the tunes and modes of singing them were handed down from one generation to the next, and variations might be developed in congregations that then became encoded in general practice. This is part of the time-honored oral tradition

---

[65] Gilbert Chase, America's Music (Urbana: University of Illinois Press, 1981), 3.

[66] Crawford, 20.

[67] Chase, 26

that would have been an essential part of our forebears' understanding of what worship should be.

In practice, only psalms were sung. "Psalm singing was first and foremost a way for members…to praise, glorify, and beg forgiveness from a just, stern, almighty God."[68] There were fewer tunes than there were psalms, but different psalms could be sung to the same few tunes. One such tune, "Old Hundred", whose origin is from the 1560s, is still sung today as the Doxology. The melody was central. There were four phrases of equal length, with the rhythm of each phrase almost identical to the others, "Stamping the whole with a unity that singers have been quick to grasp." [69] The psalms were written in standard verse forms or meter, and books were published with the psalms in these verses. These psalm books were printed without any musical notation, and it must have fallen to the choristers to lay out the tunes for the congregation to follow. The singing style emphasized the melody sung full voice. Imagine a room full of the devoted, singing a song of praise at the top of their voices. The effect must have been powerful for those in the room.

As time passed, however, an effort to reform song in worship built steam. It appears that this effort originated with clergy trained at Harvard, in the early 1700s. [70] By this time, the Puritan fervor was being diluted by the immigration of diverse populations, and the power of the clergy was beginning to give way. It's possible that the efforts to regulate singing was at least in part an effort of the clergy to assert their power in a diminishing field of influence. In any event, the Old Way singing gave way to what was known as "Regular Singing", and First Church seems to have followed suit.

The first mention of music in the church records comes in March of 1779, when Israel Judson and Daniel Sherman, Jr. were appointed choristers, along with Gideon Judson. In December of 1781 twelve pounds

---

[68] Crawford, p. 22

[69] Crawford, 23

[70] Chase, 14

10 were allocated "to promote the learning of Psalmes tunes for Divine Service", although there must have been controversy surrounding this decision, because three weeks later the decision was reversed. The same happened in 1785 when the Society voted to pay the singing master and then a month later reconsidered and decided not to. The debates that must have lain behind these votes - were there factions in the church? was it strictly economics? - can only be speculated about. Finally, according to Julia Minor Strong in her 1901 book "The Town and the People" the Society "appropriated their first music budget "…to promote the learning of psalm tunes for Divine Service," in 1781". Mrs. Strong also asserts that Josiah Judson, Stiles Curtiss, and Noah B. Benedict were appointed choristers in 1793. [71] It seems reasonable to assume that these choristers and singing masters were engaged in Regular Singing.

Regular singing helped enforce an atmosphere in the church of discipline, order, and solemnity. The parishioner became part of a body of worshippers rather than an individual voice belting out praise at the top of his or her voice. Rules took precedence over custom, and control over personal freedom. All this reflected general effort to develop and enforce rules of civility and gentility throughout society, perhaps as a collective way to try to control the growth of the population and the tremendous energy being released by immigration, independence from Britain, and innovative and entrepreneurial ways of behaving. There had to be some way of taming society and keeping order, and order within the worship service was one way to accomplish that. Remember that at this point the Church and the State were still one, and so the Church still had the mandate to assert behavioral norms.

By the 1780s Regular Singing was widely established in New England and musical literacy fairly widespread. In a town like Woodbury, which, at the time of the Revolutionary War was in the top five of Connecticut

---

[71] Larae Graham "325 Years of Music" First Congregational Church Newsletter, January 1995

towns for both population and wealth, it seems reasonable to assume that new levels of sophistication would be readily adopted, although perhaps the innate conservatism that characterized Woodbury's post war development was beginning to emerge. It wasn't until 1796 the Society voted to pay ten pounds annually to teach children to sing. "Thomas Mallory taught a singing school in the meeting room."[72] According to Crawford singing schools were widespread by the 1760s.

In 1810, $30 was to be appropriated "For the Benefit of singing and voted Noah B. Benedict, Esq., Capt. Jesse Minor, and Nathaniel Bacon a committee to lay out such money to the best advantage." In January, 1827, a committee was formed, consisting of Noah B. Benedict, Dr. R. Abernathy, and Deacon Seth Minor, to consider employing a singing teacher. In 1828 $80 was needed to be raised to pay a singing instructor for a year. The agreement was that once the money was raised, Gilbert Minor and Samuel Sherman would be hired to start a singing school. By 1832, though, it was voted inexpedient to hire any person to instruct in singing and a committee was formed to "promote singing in such ways as they shall think expedient.". In August the next year the vote was to hire a singing teacher who was a member of the society, and in September Ralph G. Camp was appointed instructor for singing. A committees formed "to advise with the Teacher in regard to the Musick and the conducting of the school". In 1834 Thomas Drakeley was appointed chorister, and in September that year $20 was to be raised to hire R. G. Camp to "Improve the singing". In December that year Thomas Mallory was made chorister. And so it continued: Ralph. Camp and Thomas Mallory seemed to be selected in tandem to direct the singing in the church for several years. In 1836 adding a room, lights, heat were added to the remit of the singing committee, and in 1839 we have the first indication of instrumental music being added "as they see fit".

---

[72] First Church Records transcript

First Church Melodeon. Photo credit S. Griswold

Adding an instrument to the music was a fairly radical move, at first. According to Gilbert Chase, country churches didn't begin to use portable instruments until the end of the 18th century. Usually that instrument was the Church Bass, a 3 -5 stringed bass viol, known as "God's fiddle to distinguish it from the Devil's fiddle."[73] Unfortunately, the church records are silent about what kind of instrumental music the singing committee "Shall judge best", but a melodeon was purchased in 1850, after Philo Trowbridge was appointed chorister.[74] Apparently there had been a small church orchestra that accompanied the choir, and the melodeon eventually replaced it. A melodeon, or reed organ, is a keyboard instrument that

---

[73] Chase, 16

[74] Larae Graham, "350 Years of Music", First Congregational church Newsletter, January, 1995

makes sound by pushing or sucking air through chambers with vibrating reed tongues.[75] At first imported and so unavailable to most people, by the 1840s they were being produced and sold by American companies, in part because European-made instruments could not withstand the climate of North America, and could not stay in tune. At the same time that the melodeon was being made, sheet music and hymn books with tunes as well as verses were being published. The singing no longer was restricted to psalms but now incorporated songwriting as we know it today.

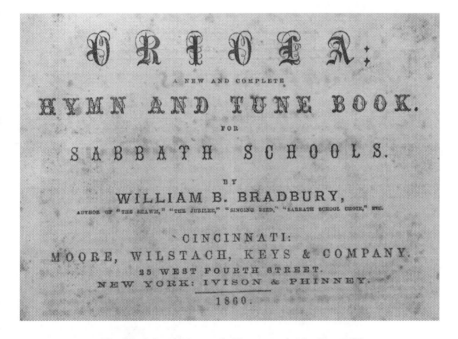

Church School Hymnal. Photo credit S. Griswold

In 1872 the Church made the final step toward a truly integrated music program that persisted for over 100 years. The church voted to purchase a Hook & Hastings Opus 170 organ selected by Deacon James H. Linsley, also the chorister. It was installed in the rear balcony in 1873. In 1897, an extension behind the pulpit was built to accommodate both

---

[75] Crawford, 234

choir and organ, and the organ was moved there. At various times it was moved again, back up to the balcony, then to the choir loft in the center, then moved to the right side of the choir loft and placed at an angle, before coming to rest in its current location, back at the center of the choir loft.

Organ in gallery, circa 1873

According to research done by Larae Graham and published in the January, 1995 newsletter, the organ was moved from the rear of the church, which was a typical location for country churches, to the front after an extension to the choir loft was built to accommodate both the choir and the organ. As Mrs. Graham writes "This was not to be its final resting place, however. In the intervening years, the instrument was moved back to the balcony(or gallery), then returned to the choir loft, in the center, then to the right side, at an angle, then again back to the center."

The first record we have of the organ being worked on comes in 1953, when the organ was being considered for a rebuild. In this record, Charles Dunn, a pipe organ expert, calls for a modern electric actions replacing outmoded tracker function. In 1968 the record picks up again. The Music Committee reported in July, 1968 that the three parts of the organ, pipes, console, and choir, are separated so that the choir can't hear, the organist plays too loudly, and the congregation can't hear the blend of the parts. In addition, the pipes and console are deteriorating. Phyllis Nininger, a long time, much beloved member of the church, the choir, and for many years the church secretary, was the Chair of the Music Committee. We are lucky that she kept copies of all correspondence regarding the organ and the deliberations of the committee. The committee engaged Mr. Aubrey Thompson-Allen to assess the organ. The report that Mrs. Nininger presented to the Council on April 18, 1968, is damning. She reports "His analysis of our organ amounts to a condemnation of it as being no longer worthy of our church. It was a good Hall tracker organ but it was ruined when it was moved and electrified." He felt that within five years the organ would be no longer playable. He recommended replacing the pipe organ and estimated that the cost would be about $16,000.

Multiple other opinions and assessments were sought. The Music Committee worked diligently to start an organ fund and research available instruments. It also sought the advice of other organ experts and churches. Richard Geddes, from Winsted, had serviced the organ since the mid-1960s. He too recommended replacing the organ, which he felt was not worth investing in beyond simple maintenance. He maintained that the electrification of the organ had essentially ruined it, along with poor materials and workmanship in former repairs. Nothing more is heard about the organ until a newspaper clipping, undated, notes that Reginald Evans of Woodbury worked on the organ.

In 1970 the old organ was moved from the rear balcony where it had been placed in 1957 back to the front of the church. Evans and his partner Everett Bassett "were hired to move and repair the organ, which has some 700 pipes made of wood or of an alloy of zinc, lead, and tin." Estimates for replacing the old organ ranged from $22,700 to $36,550 (at least $185,450 in 2019 dollars), so Evans and Bassett were hired to do the work "for around $2,900."

Evans was a recently retired engineer from Scovill, while Bassett made his living repairing cameras. Together the two men had been repairing organs in the area for about 20 years, getting their start from a love of theater organs. The newspaper article reports that the chancel of the church was "strewn with sawhorses, electric drills, and odd pieces of lumber". The men were also building the case for the pipes, apparently. Evans reported finding autographs of people on the backs of many of the organ pipes. He speculated that they were probably the people who pumped the organ in the days before there was an electric blower. The oldest date is 1866, which is curious, since there isn't a record of a pipe organ in the church before 1872. Other names were Henry S. Hitchcock, 1889, Horace "Shiner" Minor, Frank Strong, Grace Judson, and Albert C. Sherwood, all familiar surnames in the Woodbury community. Evans reported counting fifty of these autographs.

In 1971, an appeal was made to the congregation for more money for the organ, as the church was $2,300 short of the actual costs of the repairs.

Nothing further is heard until 1980, when Everett Bassett retired from maintaining the organ. Then, in 1982, the current maintenance company, The William Betts Company in Colebrook wrote Mrs. Nininger suggesting that it was again time to research alternatives to the organ. He felt that any significant expenditure of money on the organ would be a waste of money. Not mincing any words, Mr. Betts wrote "My condemnation of the organ stems from that rebuilding at which time the original mechanical action was destroyed and a very inferior action was installed in its place. The type of electric action is bad enough, but that coupled with the extremely low quality of workmanship, wiring, switching, etc. renders proper pipe speech impossible." In 1987 the organ was called a "Frankenstein, a collection of dead organs resulting in a monster" by Nicholas Thompson-Allen, who goes on to use very colorful language to further condemn the poor old organ.

By 1994, the old Hook and Hastings organ was still ailing, but the church had reached a tipping point and was prepared at last to address an almost thirty year old problem. The organ committee, chaired by Les Henchliffe, found an organ located in Yarmouth, Maine that was purchased and moved to Woodbury. The Kimball, Smallman and Frazee instrument was combined with the salvageable parts of the Hook & Hasting instrument by organist and organ builder Charles McManus, who spent months reconstructing the organ which was called "…possibly one of the finer instruments in Western Connecticut." The new organ, now called a McManis, Hook & Hastings, Kimball, Smallman and Frazee organ, was inaugurated at the 1994 town-wide ecumenical Thanksgiving service, and dedicated on January 22, 1995, in the 325th year of the church. A true labor of love, the organ continues to inspire.

Music in the 20th and 21st centuries has been an important part of church life and worship. Numerous gifted musicians have directed the choirs, played the organ, and the community of Woodbury has always been invited in to participate in concerts, special services, and other musical events. Bill Geddes, music teacher at Nonnewaug High School and founder of the Woodbury-Bethlehem Music Foundation, recalls staging Godspell in the 1990s, and remembers with great affection the annual living creche each Christmas, at which young adults and children of the church would re-enact the Christmas story with live animals and, whenever possible, a living human infant. The entire community was welcomed as they gathered round on a dark December evening to sing Christmas carols, and then repair to the Parish House for hot chocolate and refreshments.

Godspell Performance, 1993. Photo credit B. Geddes

Other memorable events have included Gospel choirs, electric guitar concerts, Baroque music, and other performances that take advantage of the great acoustics and ample seating that the church building affords.

Bell Choir, 1970s

SUNDAY SCHOOL

Sunday School Easter celebration, 1970s

From mid-Nineteenth Century on, Sunday school endured as a vital ministry of First Church, and the church devoted sizeable resources to sustaining a vital Sunday school program. The Sunday school movement was a creation of Congregationalists in the early Nineteenth Century, when the American Sunday School Union was formed in 1824, at first to teach children in cities and in the newly-emerging factory towns, in the absence of parents who were often required to work long hours. Moreover, with the disestablishment of the Congregational Church as the official religion in Connecticut (1818) and Massachusetts (1833), local public schools no longer functioned as parochial schools for the local Congregational church. Therefore, some way had to be found to provide the religious instruction that public schools no longer provided. By any measure, the Sunday schools attained considerable success. As the great historian of American religion Sydney Ahlstrom has written, "...the Sunday schools did produce a pious and knowledgeable laity on a scale unequalled anywhere in Christendom."[76]

The exact time when Sunday school began at First Church in Woodbury is undocumented, but the Nineteenth and Twentieth Century records provide us with the annual reports of Sunday school superintendents; some of these supply a rich understanding of how important First Church considered Sunday school to be and the seriousness with which Sunday school teachers approached their duties. And so important was the education of little children that the Kindergarten had its own superintendent who submitted her annual report as well. In the annual FCC report of 1870, there were 102 members, 14 teachers, and 14 independent members who did not attend classes but whose parents instructed them at home. The average attendance in 1870 was 92. Apparently members of the Christian Endeavor Society met on every other Tuesday evening, and seems to have provided many of the Sunday School teachers.[77]

From the records we have, it is evident that the content of Sunday schools underwent a change in the early twentieth century. Nineteenth Century Sunday school focused on catechism memorization for many years; the American Sunday School Union provided materials that imparted

---

[76] Sydney E. Ahlstrom, A Religious History of the American People (New haven: Yale University Press, 1972) p.742.

[77] Rev. Russell Rowland, "Celebrating 200 Years of Sunday School from Gloucester, England, to Woodbury, Connecticut" May 25, 1980,4. A typed manuscript in the FCC archives.

reformed tradition doctrine, an updated Westminster Catechism, so that students might distinguish themselves from Episcopalians and Roman Catholics. The catechisms were adjusted appropriately for different ages, with more complex explanations provided for the higher grades. This practice was aligned with Episcopalian practice, which relied heavily on the catechism found in different editions of the <u>Book of Common Prayer</u>, and presented simplified catechisms for young children. Roman Catholic religious instruction during this period relied on gradated versions of the <u>Baltimore Catechism</u>. Mrs. F.B. (Alice) O'Neill, superintendent of the Primary Class in 1933 supplies us with a vivid picture of Sunday school in her childhood in the late 19th Century and he changes wrought in the 20th Century.

"When we were very young our Sunday School teacher was an austere spinster who taught by the aid of a long black ruler- perhaps it wasn't so long—but it looked long but to our infantile eyes it looked as long as a yardstick- but may have been only a 12 inch ruler. Part of the teaching routine was the recital each Sunday of a part of the Shorter Catechism. We used to wonder why it was called "Shorter" and also if there was a longer catechism-we hoped not. No legal document we have since seen has ever appeared so voluminous as our recollections of our old catechism. Each Sunday the joy was taken out of our lives by the question "What is the chief end of man?" It was met by awed silence, but the answer was soon forthcoming from "dear teacher." "The chief end of man is to glorify God and enjoy him forever." "Now say it children" and we would try to repeat, parrot like, the words, meaningless to us, each word emphasized by a rap on the desk with the ruler so <u>not</u> to know the chief end of man would surely be the end of us. No wonder our small brother cried each Sunday, causing us untold embarrassment and fear. No effort was made to explain the meaning of the words- we just "learned" it. But who knows? Maybe it was a good method- at least we never forgot that first question- nor remembered any other, I fear. But that kind of Sunday School teaching has taken its place with tallow-dips and the covered wagon- even the name is changed- if we are really modern we have Church Schools, not Sunday Schools- the latter name dating one hopelessly. We strive now to make our Sunday School or Church a place where the children want to go, not a place where they are sent. We recently compared some quarterlies (of Sunday school materials) bearing the dates 1919 and 1920, and found the material of today more practical- there seems to be less sentimentalism- the lesson material is based more on Nature. An interest in nature helps open the child's eyes to the higher things of life. "Teach a child to love Nature and you teach him to love God" says a well-known pioneer in child education."[78]

This dramatic shift in the Sunday school curriculum would be a significant one for the entire church. No longer would the young people be brought up with a distinctive Reformed tradition theology that distinguished them from other denominations. The future of the church lay in preaching a practical morality involving the basics: love of God, love of neighbor, and fulfillment of one's Christian duty. It is difficult to assess what exactly accounts for such a change, but several things may have been at work in the early 20th Century.

First, the impact of Darwinism, and the greater tendency to look to natural, rather than supernatural causes for the day-to-day occurrences of the world cannot be overstated. Like most Protestant churches in the North, First Church allied with other more liberal, low-church evangelical churches in departing from a literal reading of Scripture. Although fundamentalists, chiefly in the South and the Midwest, continued to insist on the literal inerrancy of Scripture, New England Congregationalists allied with Northern Baptists and Presbyterians on the liberal side. If one could not discern the hand of God in the growth of each blade of grass, then, one could at least appreciate the beauty of a self-sustaining creation,

---

[78] Records of the First Congregational Church, 1921-1948, p. 117. Archives of the First Congregational Church and Connecticut State Library.

and still behold the masterwork of God in the process of evolution. And that might be the core of the Sunday school lesson.

Second, the First World War shattered Western Christendom's confidence in itself. The War had been fought at a cost of over 40 million lives. Three major empires of Europe: Germany, Russia, and Ottoman Turkey, all dismembered into a squabbling gaggle of successor states. And with the exceptions of the Ottoman Empire and Japan, all the nations that fought the War identified themselves as Christian. In the past century, all the European colonial powers had marched triumphantly into distant lands bearing the sword and the cross in the name of advancing Christian civilization. But what was one to make of Christian powers visiting such unparalleled destruction on their own civilization? Was it even possible to believe that Christianity held the key to a more peaceful future, or that armed nation states could possibly advance God's kingdom on Earth? As the 1920s advanced, Sunday schools came to emphasize the essential of the Christian life as less about doctrinal precision and more ordinary kindness. If nation-states could not be trusted to advance Christs kingdom on Earth, then perhaps that duty devolved to the individual Christian and the individual churches.

Whatever the reasons, both Darwinism and the First World War profoundly changed the landscape of American Protestantism, and First Church reflected those changes.

The Sunday school reports of the early 20th Century provide a cornucopia of information about what was taught and how students reacted to their lessons. Mrs. O'Neill provides an anecdote in her report for `1934 about one fruitful day in the early primary class:

"As our lessons progressed, obedience was the topic one Sunday, and there was Honesty, Truthfulness, Fair Play, and Property Rights with golden opportunities in each one. The lessons on obedience stressed obeying rules and laws, a wide field to be sure. After telling the children that everything is governed by a rule or law, the sunrise, the sunset, the falling leaves, school meal-time, Sunday School time, etc., we asked "Why do we have rules or laws for everything?" Barbara replied "You'd go crazy if you didn't." This seemed like a good starter, so we said "What happens when people do not obey the laws?" And said Harold "Mr. Reichenbach arrests them." That should have been the climax and finish, but since the child understands what is best nearest to him, we developed the idea of obedience from Mr. Reichenbach's activities with the law-breakers, but we were most careful to say that Mr. Reichenbach was the bogey man only to wrong-doers but our good friend every Sunday morning, for just as the children are leaving each Sunday, we caution them not to cross the street till we come out, but they say "Well, if Mr. Reichenbach is there we can cross, can't we?"[79]

The stories don't end, they just get better. In her report for 1935, Mrs. O'Neill wrote this account of one Sunday school class:

> One of our policies in teaching is to emphasize kindness and truthfulness. So we feel that if a child can be taught to play fair, to be truthful and kind, then much can be done to develop a spiritual side. So there are always sort of a hidden theme in our teaching. We have wondered just how these seeds take root and always hope for the best, but I'm afraid our bubble burst not long ago when we were addressing more particularly the older group in our lesson talk. All went well until we heard a cry and looked in the direction from whence it came, saw two of our three year olds engaged in a spirited fisticuff. We promptly removed the one we were sure was the instigator of the bout and then turned to the other to see what damage, if any, had been wrought. He said B- was a naughty boy to do that, wasn't he? We answered "Well it wasn't very kind, was it?"

---

[79] Ibid. p. 152.

"No" he replied "and when I get home I'm going to get my base-ball bat and hit him."[80]

As the 1930s wore on, the world again marched toward self-destruction, first in the Pacific with the Japanese invasion of Manchuria in 1931, the subsequent invasion of China in 1937, and the outbreak of yet another general European War in September, 1939. It must have been increasingly apparent to those Sunday school teachers that the very children they taught to love and respect others, to play fair, and deal honestly would be caught in the maelstrom of war. Unfortunately for the modern reader, leadership of the Sunday school passed into other hands and reports provided descriptions of activities but none of the insights of Mrs. O'Neill's writings. Sunday school remained highly active, but the ideas that propelled the activities, the curriculum taught, and the lively anecdotes remain largely unknown.

The World War II years, and the wide interest in unifying the First Congregational and North Congregational churches also brought opportunities to have a united Sunday school. During 1945, the two churches held three months of Sunday school programs. Apparently, the Sunday school superintendent found the experience "very gratifying," yet it was not continued.[81]

The Post-War period brought more changes in the Sunday school program. The church called on students at Yale Divinity School to further energize the program. In 1963, the Sunday school began using materials provided by the United Church of Christ, which First Church had recently joined. Unfortunately Sunday school faced a growing problem of sporadic attendance. For two years, 1966-1968, the church experimented with a home-based program with parents as the primary teachers. Apparently this satisfied few, and the program was switched back to a church-building

---

[80] Ibid. p. 164.
[81] Rowland, "Celebrating 200 Years of Sunday School" p.5

program. The middle grades-4,5,6,7-were transferred to Monday afternoon so that the children could come directly from school[82]

Sunday school in the in the 1980s and into the first decades of the Twenty-First Century years meant attending class on Sunday morning once again in the classroom spaces under the chapel. The Sunday school board worked hard to adapt to the challenges of changing demographics and Sunday morning sports to offer meaningful experiences for young families. But with essentially static population growth today and the majority (53%) of the town being 45 years old or above,[83] simply finding enough families to build an energetic Sunday school experience of any denomination is a major challenge. Consequently, as of this writing, no formal Sunday school program exists, for there are no children in the parish.

---

[82] Ibid., p.5.

[83] The median age is currently 48. CERC Town Profiles https://s3-us-west-2. amazonaws.com/cerc-pdfs/2019/woodbury-2019.pdf

THE WOMEN'S FEDERATION

All through the Twentieth Century and into the Twenty-first[t], the Women's Federation has played a crucial role in the life of First Church. Often referred to as the "backbone of the church," the Women's Federation raised funds, held programs of educational value to the church community, and worked tirelessly for the welfare of the church. For many decades, well into the 1970s, the Women's Federation oversaw an elegant coffee hour, baking, arranging for snacks, and serving coffee and tea using the church's silver and china. As an indication of the varied kinds of work that the Women's Federation engaged in, it is useful to quote from a Women's Federation Report for 1960 as fairly representative of the Federation's work over the years. Mrs. Harlan (Dorothy) Griswold, president, submitted this report for the year 1960.

Mrs. Harlan (Dorothy) Griswold, 1959

"The women's Federation has again completed a rewarding and successful year... We started this year with $1823.82 in our regular fund and $712.44 in the Reserve Fund making a total of $2536.26. We earned through the year $1685.25 and have now in the regular fund January 1, 1961 $1299.47 and in the Reserve $1021.04, making a total of $2320.51.

"We raised the money by hard work with two rummage sales, a Christmas bazaar, five food sales, sale of candy, Danny Duzit, vanilla and note paper and by collections and contributions...

"How we spent the money is of more interest than how we raised it and shows that our goals are not limited to making money for its own sake. In parting with our hard-earned funds we wanted to help our church and also reach out beyond ourselves. We spent on the Church $1106.50. We paid $300 for the Assistant Minister to Youth, Hugh Knapp, and I am sure that everyone in the Church will agree that this was a very worthwhile expenditure. ...We have spent $18.35 for flowers for the Church, $94.85 for cards for the sick and bereaved and this Christmas $30.00 for plants to shut-ins. $120.00 has been spent for equipment and cleaner for the Parish House. $15.90 for a new American flag for the Church, and $20.90 for last January's annual dinner. We sent Mrs. Ingraham to the Ministers' Wives' Conference and that cost us $15.00.

"For others we spent $384.52-To the Missionary Society of Connecticut earmarked for the Silver Lake Fund, $50.00; The Women's Second Mite Gift, $65.99; National Council of Churches for World Day of Prayer, $8.00; Retired Ministers' Fund, $50.00; and a special project this year to the U>S> Committee for Refugees, $200.00; Our Friendly Service expense was$11.22...We have also sent 200 lbs. of good clothing to Delmo Housing Corporation in Missouri and 600 lbs. of good used clothing to the U.S. Committee for Refugees. We have made a layette and done hospital sewing.

"Our telephone committee has called the Church membership ten times a total of twelve hundred calls.

"During the year we have had ten regular meetings and about fifteen sewing meetings, when the work to fill the Friendly Service quota was done and sewing for the Christmas bazaar.

Our Social committee besides helping with the covered dish luncheons which usually precede our meetings has put on three teas to which the North Church was invited…"[84]

Quietly, diligently, and prayerfully, the Women's Federation supplied many needs of the Church, and extended the good works of the church far beyond the boundaries of Woodbury.

---

[84] Dorothy Griswold, Women's Federation Report, 1960. Archives of First Church.

The Ministry At First Church

In the entire history of First Church, forty one ministers have served on either a full-time, settled basis or as an interim minister, between settled pastors. Since Volume I of this work has treated the colonial ministry quite effectively, this volume will deal only with ministers settled since 1800. A list of all ministers has been included for reference (Appendix A). But it seems important to note that the first three ministers served an average of 47 years. From the end of Rev. Mr. Noah Benedict's 53 year pastorate in 1813, no minister has held a tenure comparable in length to those of the colonial and early national eras. The longest serving pastor after 1813 was Rev. Mr. Samuel Andrews (1817-1846, 29 years). Rev. Mr. Joseph Freeman served 17 years from 1887 to 1908, and the Rev. Mr. Mark Heilshorn served twelve years from 1996 to 2008. All other pastors served less than 10 years, many for only two or three years.

The Rev. Noah Benedict. Photo credit S. Griswold

How does the modern student history make sense of these numbers? After the death of Mr. Benedict in 1813, the controversy over the location of the new meetinghouse, which had bedeviled the congregation for many years, burst forth into an open split. Apparently, Mr. Benedict skillfully kept the lid on the controversy and tried to keep all parties talking, without ever reaching a compromise. But after Mr. Benedict's passing, the next minister, Worthington Wright, realized that he had stepped into a nest with a lot of angry hornets, and he lasted only one year (1813-1814). His successor, Henry P. Strong (1814-1816), endured two tumultuous years before finding another pastorate. One faction was determined to locate the new meetinghouse near where First Church presently stands. Dissidents who wanted the church located north of the present location formed their own congregation in 1816, built their own church, and secured recognition from the State of Connecticut as the Strict Congregational Church. First Church was constructed in 1819, and the split was set in stone.

It is difficult to avoid the conclusion the split in the church weakened both churches financially, especially since the new Connecticut Constitution of 1818 deprived the churches of tax support. Both churches found it increasingly difficult to support a minister for very long. Samuel R. Andrews was the first minister at First Church to be hired after the split; he served a lengthy 29 years, but he was the last to do so. Most ministers left little in the official records about their pastoral service here beyond perfunctory pastoral reports that discussed the growth (or decline) in membership, activities during the year, and a brief exhortation for members to be more faithful in church attendance. The records unfortunately leave no real indication of how well most ministers were liked, or not. And since, in times past, difficulties with the local pastor would have been handled internally, entirely within the congregation, there is little either in church or public records about how the congregation dealt with a contentious pastoral issue.

That discrete silence came to an end in 1978, when a controversy between the Rev. Mr. Robert Wright and the Board of Deacons erupted into a public spectacle, covered extensively in the parish newsletter and in the local press. In the February, 1978, issue of the "Newsletter" Mr. Wright boldly challenged his opposition before the entire parish. He wrote:

> For several years now I have been proposing that this Church would take some actions and movement in developing programs which would aid membership growth and involvement. Among the plans I have proposed is an expansion of facilities to provide more adequate church school rooms and parish facilities such as an adequate church office, minister's study, music room, a room suitable for scouting and youth activities, a front entrance which would be more accessible to elderly and handicapped persons. I have proposed a neighborhood shepherding plan for reaching both new and existing

members, and the developing of programming of interest to persons outside the present membership, both social and of an adult education or Bible study nature.

In these proposals I have been frustrated by the general apathy of the members of this church. ...Since it is now clear to me that my effectiveness as the spiritual leader of this Church has been thwarted and there can be little hope that my leadership will, indeed, move the church forward...it is timely that I take some action.

With this in mind I have initiated my search for another position. Having conferred with Dr. Nathanael Guptill, Minister of the Connecticut Conference of the United Church of Christ at Congregational House in Hartford, at which time I asked him to circulate my Professional Profile in search of another position....This means that I will resign as Pastor of the First Congregational Church of Woodbury upon receiving a Call to another ministry..."[85]

---

[85] "Newsletter" (February, 1978), 1. Stored in the archives of First Church in the folder labelled Robert Wright.

The Rev. Robert Wright

The February, 1978 minutes of the Council meeting enabled each parish organization to provide its sentiments on the issue of Mr. Wright's resignation. The Trustees thought that Mr. Wright should submit his resignation by July 1, and that Mr. Wright should "have no ministerial duties from now on. Furthermore, Mr. Wright and his family should leave the parsonage by September 1. There was some dissention among the Deacons, but the Board voted to accept Mr. Wright's resignation as of July 15, The Christian Education Committee stated that "As a church we need to be responsive to Bob and his family in two ways: (1) by allowing Bob enough time to seek a new pastorate and move into it. (2) By supporting Bob during the remainder of his ministry with us with full vigor and involvement and by sharing leadership where needed to ensure a strong ministry during this time of transition."[86]

---

[86] Council Meeting minutes, (February 20, 1978) <u>passim.</u>

The issue dragged on into the summer, and many quiet conversations brought the church to a compromise. On July 30, Mr. Wright offered to make his resignation effective December 31, 1978, with the church paying his salary and providing use of the parsonage until that time. The Council accepted this compromise and immediately moved to create a search committee for a new pastor.[87]

The passage of time provides clarity into the past, and it is worthwhile examining the demographic factors forcing change on a reluctant Woodbury. Woodbury's population had remained roughly the same, 2000, since 1800. The Protestant churches and the town government were controlled by an interlocking network of descendants of the founders. After 1945, however, the population tripled by 1970 to just over 6000, and remained on that steep trajectory[88]. Many of the newcomers moved from cities like Waterbury and Danbury, for the opening of Interstate 84 in 1961 had made it far easier to commute to these cities for work. Professionals often sought out towns like Woodbury to get away from the noise and crowdedness of the cities, and perhaps "white flight" became a factor as well. Significantly, the majority of the newcomers didn't trace their ancestries to the Puritans seeking to build a "city upon a hill"; they were most often Roman Catholics of Irish, Italian, or Slavic extraction, with whom the old "standing order" of Woodbury had little in common. Add to all of this the larger changes in American society: the civil rights movement; the youth revolt; the growing mistrust of Americans in their own institutions after Watergate; the women's liberation movement. It must have been a frightening thing for the older, conservative, descendants of the first settlers to realize that the Woodbury of their childhood was gone, never to return, and that their days in power were numbered. In retrospect it appears that Mr. Wright attempted to open First Church more to the Woodbury community and to that changing, dynamic, wider world.

---

[87] Council Meeting minutes, (July 30, 1978), passim.

[88] https://connecticuthistory.org/wp-content/uploads/2014/03/WoodburyPop,png

His ideas of reaching out to the community for increased membership, opening up the church as a venue for more community activities may have rankled some of the older, more conservative members, particularly those in power, who may have viewed he church as a bastion of stability in a changing world. Whatever the reasons, the passage of time vindicated Mr. Wright's vision to some extent. The building projects that he envisioned, albeit somewhat scaled down, were accomplished within a few years of his departure. And Mr. Wright returned to read a poem at the 325th celebration in 1995, still esteemed by many members of the parish.

Mr. Wright was succeeded by two short term ministers, the Rev. Mr. Russell Rowland (1979-1984) and the Rev. Mr. Ronald Rising (1985-1987), before the congregation settled a much-beloved minister, the Rev. Peter Marsden. Mr. Marsden served for only seven years (1987-1994), but during his tenure he and his wife established deep roots in the local community. He is remembered for his warm, engaging, pastoral approach and his thoughtful, scripturally based sermons that applied Christian teaching to everyday life. He was sometimes asked to officiate at funerals for non-members, and he did so with great sensitivity to the families, asking them to supply information about their loved one, which he referenced in his sermon. His wife taught music in the local school system, but after her untimely death, Mr. Marsden decided to look for a call outside Woodbury. Church members still remember him fondly and recall his ministry as a time of spiritual and numerical growth for the church.

The Rev. Peter Marsden

Mention ought to be made at this point of the ministrations of the Rev. Dr. Roger Shinn, professor at Union Theological Seminary in New York and member of First Church during the summer. Mr. Shinn was a towering figure in the theological life of Protestantism. He wrote the Confession of Faith for the United Church of Christ. In his position as Reinhold Niebuhr Professor of Social Ethics at Union Theological Seminary, he influenced a generation of young clergy. The author of numerous books, Dr. Shinn figured prominently in the debates on cloning. He preached at First Church on August 2, 16, and 30, 1992, a series of sermons entitled" Three Spiritual Pilgrimages: Soren Kierkegaard, Dietrich Bonhoeffer, Dorothy Day."[89] Dr. Shinn preached on other occasions as well, on July 23rd and 30th, 1995.[90]

---

[89] Notes of Dr. Roger Shinn on Services for August 2, 16, 30. In archives of First Congregational Church

[90] Press release by Phyllis Nininger, "Roger Shinn Speaking at First Church" July 10, 1995. In archives of First Church.

The Rev. Dr. & Mrs. (Catherine) Roger Shinn

Two years passed before a successor to Mr. Marsden could be settled. In the meantime, the Rev. Mr. Stuart Brush served as interim from 1994 to 1996. Mr. Brush lived in New Milford and had served for several years of the New Preston Congregational Church before coming to Woodbury. Finally, in 1996 the congregation settled the Rev. Mr. Mark Heilshorn, a young graduate of Yale Divinity School with a wife and young children. Mr. Heilshorn's years brought considerable growth in the membership. Young families identified with Mr. Heilshorn and felt at home with his warm, informal services and colloquial sermons. The high school students involved in the Pilgrim Fellowship travelled to do building projects in high-poverty areas of the United States. But apparently anxieties developed within the congregation, and in 2008 the Council informed Mr. Heilshorn of their decision to reduce his salary. The ostensible reason was financial; as the national economy crashed during 2008 and the prospect of a serious recession loomed, stock portfolios nose-dived and lost more than half their value. Moreover, the Connecticut jobless rate would exceed ten percent, seriously impacting donations to the church. Local merchants and wage-earners struggled to survive in this atmosphere, and the economy would not recover for several years. Faced with this financial loss in salary, Mr. Heilshorn decided to resign and left the active ministry.

The Rev. Dr. Mark Heilshorn

After Mr. Heilshorn's departure, the pulpit of First Church proved difficult to fill. The Rev. Mr. Stanley Youngberg served as interim for three years (2009-2012) before a suitable applicant could be found in the Reverend Ms. Lyn Barrett, the Church's first settled woman minister. Ms. Barrett had previously served in Pennsylvania and had been associated with the German Reformed tradition within the United Church of Christ. She brought with her a liturgical tradition that was a departure from the traditional Congregationalist style of services, with a decidedly mixed reception on the part of the congregation at First Church.

The Rev. Lyn Barret

By 2015, Ms. Barrett had submitted her resignation and the congregation searched for a minister that might fit more squarely within the Congregational tradition.

The Rev. Dr. Howard Mayer

Rev. Dr. Howard Mayer came to First Church in early September 2015, for a three-month, part-time position. Fortunately, for First Church, he stayed for four and a half years, until his retirement on April 12, 2020.

During that time, Rev. Howard established great rapport with the congregation. He visited the hospital and home-bound members, presented memorial services, lovely baptisms, and delivered exceptional, evocative sermons, replete with wit, humor and inspirational messages.

A scholar and former professor of English at the University of Hartford, Rev. Howard contributed to the intellectual life at church by offering six outstanding study programs. The classes of ten to twelve people experienced a traditional Bible study; a class entitled 'Spiritual Dimensions of Contemporary Short Stories;' an Advent study group; the Bill Moyers DVD program on the Book of Genesis; one on the book of Revelation; and 'The Life and Writings of Dietrich Bonhoeffer.'

A charitable man, Rev. Howard instilled in us the attribute of sharing with the people in need. He encouraged us to participate in outreach activities and to give to the special charity drives of United Church of Christ: 'Neighbors in Need,' 'One Great Hour of Sharing,' and the 'Veterans of the Cross, Christmas Offering.'

The church deacons fondly recall being invited to a Saturday afternoon retreat at their minister's beautiful Victorian house. We all enjoyed the presenter's program and the opportunity to see Howard's award-winning garden and famous cats: Beatrice Louise and Mary Augusta.

Rev. Howard is famous for being a true Anglophile. His favorite royal is Queen Elizabeth. The congregation honored Howard at his third anniversary as minister with a party with a British motif, flags, flowers, pretty hats, sweet delicacies, and tea.

He was always helpful, especially during the difficult times, as members struggled with the problems of the church. He offered suggestions, studies and articles on church closures. He served as a role model and encouraged members to pray to God for new ideas and solutions.

Rev. Howard shares our pride in the heritage and contributions of the First Congregational Church of Woodbury, 1670-2020. At a later date, he will return to do a special worship service to commemorate our 350th anniversary.

There is a kindness, wisdom and an essence of goodness emanating from Rev. Dr. Howard Mayer. It has been a joy to have him as our pastor and friend. We thank him for his leadership and service. We wish him good health and happiness in his retirement.[91]

---

[91] Linda Osterman Hamid

Fellowship photo includes L-R Audrey Jannetty, Kathy Masiulis, Lisa Sulliman, Rev. Howard, Muffy Munson and Linda Hamid.

Linda Hamid with Rev. Howard.

Nevertheless, there is an optimistic note to be struck at this point. As of this writing, a young member of First Church is scheduled to be ordained to the ministry. Kaeley McEvoy was ordained on April 25. As Lisa Nanes-Sulliman writes:

At a young age Kaeley was religiously curious. She grew up at First Church, Woodbury and was encouraged to ask questions and seek answers. During her youth at First Church she was never told how to be a Christian, but she was able to observe models of Christian community through mission trips and late-night youth group lock-ins. She wrote her Confirmation statement of faith and thoughts about God. Her Grandma's favorite Bible verse, "I am the vine and you are the branches" (John 15:5) somewhat reminded her about the formation of the UCC. To lean into this imagery, the roots of her faith were deeply imbedded in the UCC. As we look forward to the next hundred years, as uncertain as they might be, we can feel confident the faith that our youth will carry on the works of God.

Kaeley McEvoy at her Ordination at Westmoreland Congregational
UCC in Bethesda, Maryland on April 25, 2020

The Rev Kaeley McEvoy will face formidable challenges. Young
people both nationally and in Woodbury are deserting the church in large
numbers. When young families move into town, they often decide not to
look for a church and become, in effect, "unchurched" as Sunday morning
soccer has often replaced Sunday morning worship. Protestant churches are
hit especially hard. Certainly, attendance at Roman Catholic churches has
dipped seriously during these times, especially in the wake of the pedophilia
scandals that plagued the Roman Church. This resulted in the closure
and consolidation of many urban parishes that could no longer afford to
maintain the massive architectural masterpieces constructed by immigrant
congregations at the turn of the 20th Century. But Protestant churches are
generally much smaller in membership and therefore more vulnerable than
Roman Catholic churches; the loss of a handful of parishioners could mean

reducing the pastor's position to part-time and curtailing vital programs. Once this happens, and once there are too few children for a Sunday school, the church is sailing in perilous waters. Today, scores of United Church of Christ, Episcopal, and Methodist churches in Connecticut are in serious trouble. For example, the First Congregational Church of Danbury sold their magnificent, Georgian-revival meetinghouse to the town of Danbury and now rents the building for services. The First Congregational Church of Litchfield, Lyman Beecher's church, has a part-time pastor, obviously not a good sign. Sixty percent of Episcopal churches in Connecticut do not have a full time rector or priest-in-charge. Many have part time ministers or use "supply" clergy. This includes many notable and architecturally significant churches such as St. John's in Waterbury and St. John's in Washington.

So what can one say about the abiding value of First Church today? Even burdened by difficulties of reduced membership numbers and finances, First Church has played a key role in the Woodbury community: negotiating the culture wars by creating an atmosphere, or culture, of acceptance of multiple points of view as society at large has become more polarized. Sometimes the effect of that has been to create the appearance of not taking any kind of position-which can aggravate both sides of a world view- but when it works it is one of the few places in modern society where one can rub shoulders, and indeed worship, with people who have very different perspectives. According to one life-time member, "That is one of the things I valued about First Church-I appreciated hearing different points of view other than the ones that reinforced my own prejudices. Alas, I don't think that there's much room these days for that kind of association. Everyone seems to want reside in an echo chamber that supports their own point of view (including me)."[92]

---

[92] Sarah K. Griswold

CELEBRATIONS

As the church that founded Woodbury, the members of First Congregational Church have always been aware of this important heritage. For the first two hundred years, though, the townspeople and church members were more likely to be engaged in doing the work of the church than reflecting on and celebrating it. Establishing homes, farms, and industry, educating the young, building the church, and sending out soldiers to war or missionaries to areas needing Christian guidance, took the time and attention of the membership. If there were anniversary celebrations and thanksgivings, the records of them have been lost or were not considered worthy of note. As the 19th century progressed, however, technological inventions and a more consumer-focused economy were introduced making daily life significantly easier. The Civil War, too, with its devastating loss of life and threats to the stability of the republic, changed the tenor of the times. We see celebrations and the erection of memorials starting around the country at this time. Woodbury was no different.

William Cothren, Esq.

No history of Woodbury or First Church can be complete without a mention of William Cothren. Born and educated in Maine in 1819, Cothren was the son of good New England stock and a paragon of this new social awareness. He went to college and studied law in Maine, moved to Woodbury in 1844, studied law again under Hon. Charles B. Phelps in Woodbury, and was admitted to the bar of Litchfield County in 1845. In 1847 he received a Master of Arts degree from Yale. His adopted town of Woodbury, where he practiced law for the remainder of his life, became his passion. According to the *Illustrated Popular Biography of Connecticut* "He ranks among the leading lawyers of the state. As a citizen he has ever been public spirited and generous. He has lent his voice and pecuniary aid to every monument or other public improvement during his time."[93]

---

[93] The Illustrated Biography of Connecticut (Hartford: J. A. Spalding Press of the Case, Lockwood & Brainard Co., 1891)

He married in 1849 and joined First Church in 1850. An organizer of the Republican Party, he was "somewhat active in its interests." [94] During the Civil War he was a supporter of the Union cause, and he was active in genealogical and historical societies as well as an active writer of prose and verse. In 1854 he published a three volume history of Woodbury, a book that he updated into the 1870s and that still remains the definitive history of the town. It is an invaluable repository of data, stories, and legends. In 1859 he organized a Bi-centennial of the Town, although that date reflected a rather specious historical fact, since it refers to a purchase of property that may or may not have happened, and that, whatever the facts of the case, would have meant something quite different to the indigenous people already thriving here than it did to the colonialists.

The 1859 celebration, elaborate and laudatory, with all the bunting and garlands, speechifying and gathering and eating that a Victorian community could want, paved the way for the Bicentennial Celebration of the Church eleven years later in 1870. In both cases, there is a triumphal, self-congratulatory quality to the celebrations, with the added sense, five years past the Civil War, of a people on the right side of history. Because Cothren was a writer, the 1870 celebration was printed as a report that includes the schedule of events and transcripts of the remarks and poetry that were shared.

Preparations were begun in September, 1869 with a vote at the annual meeting. As Cothren puts it in the published report "It was believed to be well to set up a monument to mark the passage of the ages. It was thought fitting that the Church, which had for two hundred years, acknowledged the same confession of faith, and "owned the same covenant" written and adopted by the fathers by the shores of Long Island Sound, taken "from out the Word" should, with devout joy and thanksgiving, render praise to Almighty God for all His wonderful mercies toward it. We could do no less than to render thanks to the Lord. It seemed to redound to His

---

[94] I*bid.*

glory and our great good." [95] There were committees. The Committees of Decoration and Floral Decoration fell to the ladies, while the gentlemen were in charge of the Finance and Refreshments committees. Henry C. Curtis of Hartford, Connecticut, was hired as the Decorative Artist.

Sanctuary Decorations 1879 Centennial

The program itself started at 10:00 AM, with scripture reading, hymn singing, a sermon, a prayer and a benediction; a short, five minute recess, and

[95] William Cothren, "Report of the Bi-Centennial Jubilee of the First Congregational church,"(J. H. Benham & son, Printers, New Haven, 1870)

then a communion service. Forty Five minutes were allowed for a collation recess held at Town Hall, and then there was a dedication of the new Fathers' Monument in the cemetery at 12:45. Back at the church starting at 1:45 PM and probably lasting for the remainder of the day, were singing, prayers, greetings, "sentiments" offered by the ministers of the mother church and the daughter churches, each sentiment set off from the others by singing, and then concluding with the reading of letters from former members and pastors who were unable to attend the gathering. The concluding prayer was led by Rev. G.W. Noyes of First Church, who also delivered a benediction. The speeches and sermons, presented in the florid and to our modern ear, sentimental, Victorian prose extolled the founding fathers, told the stories of settlement, and the numbers of members added to the church rolls under each minister. Reverend Noyes' sermon is worth quoting in part:

> To the wise effort, bright example, fervent prayers, of these men, the church is greatly indebted for its unity, stability and success. Society has received more marvelous modifications in these two centuries than in any other two since the Christian era. In this period, printing, steam, machinery, electricity, have been exerting their magic and civilizing power. In this period, too, gradually, indeed, church edifices have improved in style and comfort. Square pews, eagle-nest pulpits, with sounding boards, have disappeared. The worshipers rent their seats, and are not seated as formerly, according to age and rank. The cold, humid air, which our fathers and mothers endured for hours is rarified by the heat of stove or furnace. About the sanctuary no Sabbath-day houses appear; and instead of coming to church on foot, or upon saddles or pillions, as of old, the people now come in spring wagons or covered carriages."[96]

---

[96] *Ibid*, 22

Rev. Noyes ends by saying "When the next century comes round, and posterity gathers for commemoration, what shall be the aspect of the place, and the character of the people?"

Other Nineteenth Century celebrations were more ephemeral, more light-hearted. The church has in its archives flyers for various fetes and parties; a Humpty Dumpty party, fundraisers, ice cream socials, and other events, all attesting to a vibrant and lively community of people thoroughly engaged in their town and church. But the 1870 celebration started a tradition of commemorating the longevity of the church that has persisted throughout the 150 years since.

The Twentieth Century brought First Church many opportunities for celebration, and these were just as much a celebration of Woodbury as a community as celebrations for First Church. Congregationalist in emphasis, yet ecumenical in character, these celebrations commemorated milestones in the church's history and major undertakings.

The Church observed the 250th anniversary of its founding on May 5, 1920, with festive morning and afternoon services presided over by the Rev. Raymond A. Fowles, pastor from 1917 to 1922. The morning service included Communion, administered by Mr. Fowles, assisted by former pastors, the Reverend Mr. Stanley F. Blomfield (pastor, 1905-1908) and the Rev, Mr. Robert F. Davis (pastor, 1915-1917). Other neighboring ministers, the Rev. Mr. F. H. Sawyer, the Rev. Mr. C.H. Beers, and the Rev. Mr. J.L.R. Wyckoff contributed the pastoral prayer, the scripture reading, and the benediction. The afternoon service, at 2 o'clock, involved prayer, scripture, and three addresses, one by the Rev. Mr. R. C. Whitehead, the second by the Rev. Mr. Edward Noyes, and the third by Mr. Floyd Hitchcock. Delegates from each of the daughter churches (Roxbury, Washington, Bethlehem, Southbury, South Britain, and North Church) provided five-minute addresses each, according to the program for the day. Perhaps the anniversary committee limited the time to five minutes each because the addresses from daughter churches at the two hundredth anniversary celebration in 1870 took well more than five minutes each. Apparently, attention spans had begun to shorten; yet one marvels still at how the congregation sat quietly for over two hours through the many addresses.[97]

Just seven years later, the church leaders decided upon a major renovation of the meetinghouse, and the work was completed by the time of the rededication service on November 11, 1928. As with previous celebrations, the church held both morning and afternoon services presided over by the Rev. Mr. Clinton Wilson (pastor, 1925-1932). The old pulpit, which had been originally constructed in 1857 and removed some time later, was restored to its prominent position. Mr. Wilson led the congregation in reciting the prayer of consecration. After the singing of "America," Mr. Fowles' address, "The Church and the Nation," emphasized that the pulpit had been in place during the Civil War and that the day also commemorated the 10th anniversary of the Armistice that ended the fighting in the World War. Mrs. Goodrich Smith sang a solo, "Christ in Flanders" to remember the veterans of the War:

Have you seen him in the fields of Flanders with his brave and tender smile?

Did he ease your load on that shell-swept road on that last, long, weary mile?

Did you meet him among your comrades and in distant lands?

In the Sun's red glare did you see Christ there, with the heart of France in his hand?[98]

---

[97] "250th Anniversary First Congregational Church Woodbury, Conn." Program of the day archived at the First Congregational Church.

[98] YouTube.com/watch?v=3QGnFqWEeSO

Mr. Wilson then dedicated the memorial font in honor of Deacon Matthew Minor, Deacon from 1793 to 1835, given by his descendants. Over forty of those descendants were present, and the pastor reminded the congregation that over two-thousand people had been baptized or received into the church since its founding.[99] The congregation appropriately sang the hymn "Faith of our Fathers" before the benediction. At the 2 o'clock afternoon service, Pastor Wilson presented the story of the founding and early years of First Church from its origins in Stratford. The Rev.Mr. George Johnson of the First Congregational Church in New Milford, representing the Litchfield South Association of Congregational Churches, presented an address on "The Church." The Rev. Mr. Tertius Van Dyke delivered greetings collectively from the six daughter churches, and the service concluded with the consecration of the new vestibule light, given in memory of Annie Bradley Johnson by Mr. and Mrs. Allen W. Johnson.[100]

Deacon Matthew Minor Font erected 1928

[99] Records of the First Congregational Church, 1921-1949. Manuscript archived at the First Church and at the Connecticut State Library, Hartford, 71

[100] "First Congregational Church Woodbury, Connecticut, Special Services Sunday, November 11, 1928" Program for the day archived at the First Congregational Church, Woodbury.

The interwar period gave Americans, and Europeans as well, the chance to reflect on the War, and its cost in human lives and property. Virtually no one thought that the results of the War had been worth the astounding loss of life: up to 19 million military and civilian deaths and 23 million wounded. The War had been an egregious waste of men and resources. Christian churches, moreover, had to reckon with the realization that the European powers who considered themselves Christian nations had wrought this terrible destruction on their own civilization. When World War II broke out, many Christians began to think that denominational differences were far less important than the central message of Christ to love God and fellow people. Christians, therefore, needed to present a united front to accomplish that mission. During wartime, all the Protestant Churches in Woodbury (First Congregational, North Congregational, Woodbury Methodist, and St. Paul's Episcopal) held union services from January through March, rotating among the different church buildings.

The end of World War II coincided with First Church's 275th anniversary and attempts to reunite First Church and North Church. Each church appointed members of a joint committee to explore unifying the churches. Under the proposal, both meetinghouses would be used, each for half the year, with churches consolidating staff. The new name would be either The United Congregational Church of Woodbury or the Congregational Church of Woodbury.[101] In this heady atmosphere First Church celebrated its 275th anniversary, with North Church joining in the morning service. Both ministers officiated at the Communion service and the two congregations recited a joint Affirmation of Faith. At the afternoon service, modeled after previous commemorations, Governor Raymond E. Baldwin delivered remarks. Apparently discussions went on the next two years, for the next mention of unification efforts is in 1947. The church held a meeting on September 25 to discuss and vote on unification, but the vote ended up 34 "no" and 30 "yes." Several church members expressed

---

[101] "Records of the First Congregational Church of Woodbury, 1921-1949, 243

interest that the committee on unification continue its work, but several key members resigned.[102]

Nothing more was heard of the matter until 1976, when the Board of Deacons of both churches met together to consider the union of the two churches once again. This was after a summer seminarian had done a survey of the religious climate in Woodbury, which concluded that "In these times of dispersion the churches are no longer the focus of community projects and ideals." The project had been prompted by the increasing heterogeneity of Woodbury, "the summer breakdown of the churches, the winter weekend breakdown of the churches, and ... the people who call on the churches only for birth, marriage, sickness, and death. We suspect that the churches merely serve socially respectable functions, that they merely elicit the reflex actions learned in past decades."[103] What seminarian David Smucker had uncovered was that the rapid secularization of society in the 1960s and 1970s had reached Woodbury. This development would ultimately diminish the membership rolls of many churches, and, in the past two decades, force many to close. There is scarcely a town in Connecticut that has not seen church closings, mergers, and the repurposing of church buildings for secular uses. This trend has proceeded especially rapidly in New England, although other regions of the United States have been affected as well.[104] At any rate, despite the diaconates of both churches approving a merger, and the actual

---

[102] Records of the Meeting September 25, 1947 in the archives of the First Congregational Church.

[103] David Smucker, Concluding Report on the Student Summer Service Project, 1973, in the archives of the First Congregational Church.

[104] Robert Wuthnow, <u>After the Baby Boomers: How Twenty and Thirty Somethings Are Shaping the Future of American Religion</u> (Princeton: Princeton University Press) *passim.*

appointment of a subcommittee to present a proposal to the councils of both churches,[105] the effort once again failed to gain approval.

Although unable to achieve a union of the two local churches, First Church nevertheless pressed on and looked to unity on a more national level. Many churches were merging in the 1950s: the Presbyterians, split over slavery before the Civil War into Northern and Southern branches, combined to form the Presbyterian Church of the U.S.A... Northern and Southern Methodist churches united in a similar way to form the United Methodist Church. In 1957, the German Evangelical and Reformed Church, which had a Calvinist lineage and a strong base of support in Pennsylvania and the Midwest, combined with the Congregational Christian Churches of New England to form the United Church of Christ.[106] In step with most of her sister churches, including North Church, the First Church formally voted to unite with the United Church of Christ on July 4, 1961.[107] The move was not accomplished without opposition, however. A minority felt that the church might lost its distinctive local, congregational character by joining a national body. Some dissenters left their churches and formed Congregational churches outside the United Church of Christ, such as in Harwinton, where a schism led to a separate Founders Congregational Church that exists today. Fortunately for First Church, Woodbury, the dissenters reconciled themselves to the union and did not pursue a schismatic course.

Within the First Church itself, consolidation continued when the First Ecclesiastical Society, which had governed the fiscal affairs of the church since its founding, voted to merge with the Church Council, thus

---

[105] Memorandum to the Councils of First Congregational Church and North Congregational Church from the deacons of both churches, April 30, 1976 in the archives of the First Congregational Church

[106] Ahlstrom, 753-755.

[107] First Church Chronology, 16. A typed manuscript in the archives of the First Church, Woodbury.

eliminating the confusing, and at times contentious, relationship between the two bodies.

From time to time, First Church held a service on "Founders Day, May 5, with a service at Bethel Rock on a date in May. One description of a Founders Day service survives from May 24, 1955, when the church held a worship service at 8 a.m. at Bethel Rock and a reception at First Church afterwards. The service included the hymns "Faith of Our Fathers," "Fairest Lord Jesus," and "O God, Our Help in Ages Past." The minister preached on a verse from Genesis (28; 16-19) "And Jacob...said, surely the Lord is in this place...And he called the name of that place Bethel."[108]

Bethel Rock, ca. 1860

By the 300th Anniversary of First Church in 1970, the church was ready to publish a pictorial directory of the parish. Parish minister Robert W. Wright wrote that "Each Christian Church is meant to be a community, a Christian Family called by Christ to express in its own neighborhood the Good News, the Christian way of life, and to do its share in His

---

[108] 285th Anniversary Service at Bethel Rock. A typed manuscript in the archives of First Church, Woodbury.

wider mission to the world." At that time the church had 240 members in the environs of Woodbury but an equal number of members at greater distances from the meetinghouse who remembered the church fondly and kept ties to their home community.[109]

The final opportunity for the church to celebrate in the 20th Century was the 325th Anniversary, observed in 1995, under the interim pastorate of the Rev. Mr. Stuart Brush. Each of the daughter churches provided heir pastors for a reflection on their origins from First Church. Former pastor Reverend Mr. Robert Wright read a special poem for the occasion written by Clarence Stiles, entitled "A Place in the Woods."

Here, then, beneath the Greenwood shade,
The Pilgrim first his altar made;
'Twas here amid the mingled throng,
First breathed he prayer and woke the song.
How peaceful smiled that Sabbath sun,
How holy was that day begun,
When here amid the dark woods dim,
Went up the Pilgrims' first low hymn!
Look now upon the same still scene,
The wave is blue the turf is green;
But where are now the wood and wild,
The Pilgrim and the forest child?
The wood and wild have passed away;
Pilgrim and forest child are clay;
But here upon their graves we stand,
The children of that Christian band.[110]

---

[109] "First Congregational Church...300th Anniversary, 1670-1970, Pictorial Directory" Published in 1970 and in the archives of First Church.
[110] "First Congregational Church of the United Church of Christ 325th Anniversary." Pamphlet in the archives of First Church, Woodbury.

Now we celebrate the 350th Anniversary of First Church, but the celebration is bittersweet. First Church now has fewer than fifty active members; because of declining membership and little prospect of revivifying the church, the membership has voted to suspend public worship and other activities. First Church will still exist as a legal entity holding the church property, but the history of First Church as a living, worshipping Christian community, has drawn to a close for the moment.

First Congregational church. Photo Credit M. Platt

TOWARD THE FUTURE

"When the next century comes round, and posterity gathers for commemoration, what shall be the aspect of the place, and the character of the people?"

The Reverend Gurdon Noyes could have had no idea, when he spoke these words in 1870, of the changes that were in store for his community, though he may have had intimations of changes ahead. Although the next century he was talking about was only thirty years distant, even between 1870 and 1900 tremendous changes were underway, with more to come. Now, one hundred fifty years following celebration of the 200th anniversary of the church, our community has seen two devastating world wars, including the detonations of the atom bomb and the world changing implications of living in a nuclear world; smaller, endless conflicts of every kind around the globe, and devastations to the environment that could not have been anticipated in the hopeful 19th century. The industrial age that was already underway in its transformations of economies, moralities, and social and educational structures, seemed a boon to mankind then, though even in 1870 there were hints of the challenges to come from an industrialized society. The concept of a world where communications could be instantaneous, where easy global travel was limited only by one's economic resources, where population growth and diversity would lead both to greater understanding as well as increased strife; the broadening of awareness of other religions, social norms, cultural mores, and the

99

challenges and opportunities that this broadening has given us, would have been hard to imagine in 1870. The changes in attitudes toward the people our English forebears displaced, the moral implications of treating indigenous peoples around the world as 'savages' might be hard for Rev. Noyes and his congregation to understand were they to return. The changing roles of women, societal attitudes about sexual and gender identity and behaviors, social class and hierarchy, all had their roots in Rev. Noyes' day, but he and his congregation would never have anticipated them. Our world has grown infinitely more complex in so many ways, and our understanding of what it means to be human has consequently changed.

The difficulties in our own times of grappling with that change on individual as well as community levels affects us all. Science has called the nature of God into question at the same time that the Great Questions and discoveries about the nature of the physical universe suggest that it is not God that has changed, but, perhaps, our understanding that God is of a greater nature than any of us can really grasp, and is truly beyond any conventional understanding. In the end, we are forced back to the mysteries of our existence in a universe that is both embodied and disembodied, or in other words both physical and spiritual. Our Congregational tradition still provides us ways of understanding and behaving morally in this infinitely complex world, but the means by which we understand and practice our tradition must change, as it has continually since the very beginning of the Puritan revolution.

The suspension of Sunday worship and the prospect of a pastor-less church opens up new and different possibilities for First Church. Could a small number of congregants meet on a weekday evening for a lay-led Bible Study? Could a Bible study of this nature eventually be opened to the public? Could the small group bring in a minister for an occasional Communion? Could the Church rent space elsewhere in a busy, commercial area to serve as outreach? Could First Church provide speakers for the public, which might present different sides of a thorny current issue, each with a Christian perspective? Could the meetinghouse serve as a venue to present concerts featuring the best music of many faith traditions? Could a local theater group find a home in First Church? The possibilities are virtually endless, and it lies within the power of the membership at First Church to determine the future.

In our UCC tradition we say "God is Still Speaking". We believe that the suspension of traditional Sunday worship means that if we are careful to listen, we will hear what God has in store for us for the next 350 years.

Appendix 1: Ministers of First Church

Zecheriah Walker, 1670-1700

Anthony Stoddard, 1702-1760

Noah Benedict, 1760-1813

Worthington Wright, 1813-14

Henry P. Strong, 1814-16

Samuel R. Andrews, 1817-46

Lucius Curtiss, 1846-54

Robert G. Williams, 1855-59

Charles G. Robinson, 1861-64

Charles Little, 1865-67

Horace Winslow, 1868-69

Gurdon Noyes, 1869-79

A.W. Colver, 1879-82

Alfred G. Powelson, 1882-86

Joseph A. Freeman, 1887-1905

Stanley Blomfield, 1905-08

Howard A. Seckerson, 1908-11

W.H. Harris, 1911-12

R. Arnold Schackleton,1912-15

Robert H. Davis, 1915-17

Raymond A. Fowles, 1917-22

Fred W. Shorter, 1922-23

Daniel P. Hatch, 1923-24

Clinton W. Wilson, 1925-32

Rolland W. Ewing, 1932-38

William Hawkes, 1938-47

Joseph Loughran, 1948-51

John P. Cranston, Jr., 1952-57

Robert W. Ingraham, 1958-60

Leslie W. Blandon, 1961-63

Eben T. Chapman, 1963-68

Robert W. Wright, 1969-78

Elizabeth and Donald Fraser (Interim), 1978-79

Russell Rowland, 1979-84

Ronald A. Rising, 1985-87

Peter V. Marsden, 1987-94

Stuart Brush (Interim), 1994-96

Mark L. Heilshorn, 1996-2008

Stanley E. Youngberg (Interim) 2009-12

Lyn Barrett, 2012-15

Howard Mayer, 2015-20

APPENDIX 2

The Rev. Samuel Andrews, ca. 1846

The Rev. Joseph Freeman,, ca. 1890

The Rev. A. W. Colver, ca. 1880

The Rev. Stanley Blomfield & Family, ca. 1905

The Rev. R. Arnold Shakleton, ca. 1915

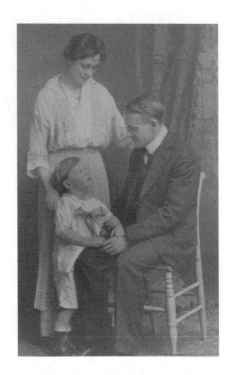

The Rev. Shakleton & Family

The Rev. Raymond A. Fowles, ca. 1920

APPENDIX 3: CHURCH LIFE

left to right: Liz Jaffin, Larae Graham, Linda Osterman Hamid
Women's Fellowship Christmas Fair

left to right: Helga Weed, Larae Graham, Kathy Masiulis,
Dorothy Winn, Audrey Jannetty, Muffy Munson
Annual Christmas Fair

Confirmands Leading Worship, 2013

2016 Congregation.. Photo Credit Liz Jaffin

Women's Fellowship Luncheon, 2016
Names left to right. Front row - Helga Weed, Kathy Buck,
Audrey Jannetty, Joan Bengtson, Dorothy Winn, Kathy
Masiulis, Linda Osterman Hamid, Muffy Munson.

l-r: Maria Platt, Rev. Howard Mayer, Ellie Swanson, Cliff Swanson.

Third Anniversary Celebration for Rev. Dr. Howard Mayer 2018
Left to rt. Larae Graham, Joan Bengston, Muffy Munson,
Sandy Green, Kathy Masiulis, Marcia Pattillo, Rev. Howard
Mayer, Linda Osterman Hamid, Liz Jaffin, Helga Weed

Third Anniversary Celebration for Rev. Dr. Howard Mayer 2018
Left to rt. Ken Green, Ed Masiulis, Mike Crowe, Rev. Howard Mayer,
Dave Jaffin, Matt Minor, Cliff Swanson, Dave Sonnemann

APPENDIX 4: A FEW
NOTABLE PEOPLE

John Fleming, Proud Democrat in a Republican town, Decades-
long member, and initiator of the Youth Recognition Fund

Skip Jaret, Founder, Organizer, and Chief Cook for the
annual Community Free Thanksgiving Dinner

Women's Retreat, 2011

Doug Schlicher, Sexton

Church Staff, 2000. L-R: Dale Krupnik (Red Barn Manager),
Rev. Mark Heilshorn, Barbara Soderberg (Music Director),
John Craft (Soloist), Maria Platt (Office Manager)

Mr. Bartlett, Stalwart member and supporter, who with his
wife Dot, took care of nearly everything, at 104 years old

Kimiyo (Kimi) Zaima, 102

Eric & Karen Walker, 9th great grandson of Rev. Zechariah Walker

Phyl Nininger, Office Manager, Music Committee Chair

Norm Taylor, a longtime member who was Moderator of the Church
at one time and on numerous Boards, Committees and in the Choir.

APPENDIX 5: WHO'S WHO AT FIRST CHURCH

STAFF

Pastor:	The Rev. Dr. Howard Mayer
Office Administrator:	Maria Platt
Organist/Choir Director:	Sandy Mehinovic
Red Barn Thrift Shop Manager:	Mary MacLeod
Sexton:	Doug Schlicher

COUNCIL MEMBERS:

Moderator:	Liz Jaffin
Assistant Moderator:	Open
Christian Education Coordinator:	Virginia Garms and Liz Jaffin
Clerk of the Church:	Helga Weed
Communications Coordinator:	Mary MacLeod
Deacon Coordinator:	Matt Minor
Deacon Representative:	Linda Osterman Hamid
Financial Coordinator:	Virginia Garms
Financial Secretary:	Bonnie Gardella
Historian:	OPEN
Outreach Coordinator:	OPEN
Properties/Trustees Coordinator:	Ken Green
Treasurer:	Roberta O'Neil
Member-at-Large:	Matt Minor

WOMEN'S FELLOWSHIP

Joan Bengtson, Kathy Buck, Marcia Pattillo- Crowe, Lynn
Erbe, Bonnie Gardella, Rachel Gerowe, Larae Graham,
Sandy Green, Sarah Griswold, Bette Gurry,
Terri Hale, Linda Osterman Hamid, Liz Jaffin, Audrey Jannetty, Kathy
Masiulis, Muffy Munson, Lisa Sulliman, Roberta O'Neil, Muriel St.
Pierre, Ellie Swanson, Helga Weed, Cindy Wiltshire, Kimi Zaima

350th ANNIVERSARY COMMITTEE

Linda Osterman Hamid, Chair, Audrey Jannetty,
Kathy Masiulis, Marcia Pattillo

First Congregational Church
214 Main Street South
Woodbury, Connecticut 06798

Office Phone: 203-263-2846
Office Email: mail@firstchurchwoodbury.org
Website: www.firstchurchwoodbury.org

~ 2 ~

Printed in the United States
By Bookmasters